THE LUMINARY CODE

HOW LEADERS TRANSFORM TECH COMPANIES INTO CUSTOMER-CENTRIC POWERHOUSES

ROAJER GILBERT

The Luminary Code: How Leaders Transform Tech Companies into Customer-Centric Powerhouses

PREFACE

Greetings readers! I'm Roajer Gilbert, author of the book you're holding, The Luminary Code: How Leaders Transform Tech Companies into Customer-Centric Powerhouses.

As a business architect with over 20 years in technology, I've been an insider guiding companies through major transformations. Change is never easy, especially for established organizations. People cling to the familiar. Pushing too hard creates resistance.

Leaders need courage, vision, and commitment to inspire teams out of their comfort zones. They must spark that spirit of innovation and change we all have inside, if it's nurtured effectively.

That's why I wrote this book using the fictional story of Holt Technologies, led by courageous CEO Aldy. When he realizes they need to overhaul their business model to meet changing customer demands, he stirs up a ruckus, trying to shift their sales approach to solution selling.

As you can imagine, trying to do things differently gets his people riled up! Aldy perseveres through many bumps to steer Holt towards reinvention.

I chose a narrative format because stories stick with me more than lectures. I hope it helps the readers to complete the book as they learn some complex business frameworks and strategies.

By experiencing Holt's very human challenges firsthand, the lessons become more visceral. You'll relate to the range of reactions from Aldy's team—skepticism, discomfort, but also growing excitement.

At its core is Aldy's discovery of 10 key principles—the Luminary Code—to lead through uncertainty. Things like:

- Customer-centricity: Obsess over current and future needs

- Fostering innovation and prudent risk-taking

- Communicating with honesty and transparency

- Driving a results-focused culture

But lofty principles mean little without living them when it counts most. Following Holt's journey makes the Luminary Code resonate deeply.

Aldy builds a framework called Neoteric to pilot transforming Holt into a customer-centric solutions company. This tale aims to inspire readers with a model for change. A framework also helps you, readers, adapt to this change in your current organization in a structured way.

I believe any company can transform with courage, resilience, and commitment to core values as their compass. This underdog story aims to stir your spirit. Let Holt ignite your own inner change agent!

So buckle up for their wild ride of reinvention! Immerse yourself in Holt's challenges, insights, and small wins that ultimately lead to victory. Enjoy the journey, and let it kindle your passion to take your own organization to new heights!

CONTENTS

DOGS NOT BARKING

THE HIDDEN THREAT WITHIN

I n the heart of Silicon Valley, where innovation breathed through the very air, the leadership team of Holt gathered around a polished mahogany table that reflected the glow of overhead lights. The sleek and modern conference room at the Palo Alto headquarters buzzed with a muted tension, an anticipation of change that had yet to take form.

Aldy, at the head of the table, surveyed his team: Anto's sharp gaze flickering over financial summaries, Audrey's poised figure leaning into the conversation, Tony's meticulous notes brimming with data points, and Christina's thoughtful eyes considering each word spoken.

Aldy cleared his throat, glancing at the graphs projecting on the wall. "I don't have a good story to tell the board this time," he began, his voice carrying a weight that demanded attention. "Our reports are good; they are as expected, which is almost flat growth."

Audrey raised an eyebrow, her lips curving into a half-smile that didn't quite reach her eyes. "Is that bad?" she questioned. The room fell silent for a moment as all eyes turned towards Aldy.

Anto leaned back in her chair, folding her arms as she scrutinized Aldy. "Steady as she goes isn't usually cause for alarm," she added, her voice even but laced with curiosity.

Aldy nodded slowly. "Steady doesn't win races in our industry. We're not sinking, but we're not soaring either."

Tony tapped his pen against his notepad before interjecting. "It's about momentum," he said. "The market won't wait for us to catch up if we're only maintaining pace."

Christina folded her hands on the table, her voice calm yet firm. "If we're not advancing, we might as well be retreating," she chimed in.

The room absorbed their collective acknowledgment of an unspoken truth: standing still was akin to falling behind in their relentless industry. The flicker of shared understanding sparked a silent resolve among them; change was imminent.

Aldy lifted his glass, the water catching the light from the panoramic windows lining one wall of the conference room. He took a slow sip, then set it down with precision that matched his tailored suit and perfectly knotted tie. His eyes wandered beyond the glass, where the city's tech temples sprawled in the distance.

"You all know our story," Aldy began, his voice steady, resonating with the kind of certainty that had carried him to the helm of Holt. "We didn't just stumble into this industry; we were born from a vision. John Holt saw tomorrow's needs etched in the tech-starved landscape of yesterday."

His gaze returned to the room, sweeping across faces etched with varying degrees of concern and anticipation. "Holt began as a system integrator, but we were more than just assemblers—we were pioneers. Our core business thrived on innovation, on delivering solutions before they were sought after."

He paused, allowing his words to settle among the collection of thoughts brewing in his audience. "For thirty years, that foresight set us apart. We became leaders not by chance but by choice—John's choice to build something enduring."

Aldy's eyes commanded the attention of the room, his tone turning reverent as he encapsulated the essence of their founder. "John Holt's vision wasn't just ahead of its time—it crafted our time," he said tersely. "He saw the raw potential in tech integration, envisioning solutions that would set the cornerstone for an industry on the brink of explosion."

He leaned in, voice low and compelling. "This wasn't just about piecing together parts; it was about pioneering paths, carving our niche in a future we defined. He believed innovation was our lifeblood, our mandate—not merely an option but our imperative."

"John taught us that adaptability and foresight were the hallmarks of a leader. He built something to last; a legacy that's ours to uphold. It's that enduring spirit, that drive for excellence, that must guide our course now. We don't just owe it to him—we owe it to ourselves." Aldy's words came to rest with a steely resolve, crystallizing the lineage of ambition that Holt was built upon.

The reflection of ambition shone in Aldy's eyes as he leaned forward slightly. "He laid a foundation on which we've built empires of progress, on thinking bigger than big. That legacy," he tapped a finger against the mahogany for emphasis, "is our compass in this ever-shifting market."

Aldy's gaze swept across the sleek conference room, pausing to rest on the faces of his leadership team. His voice, usually steady and commanding, carried a note of vulnerability as he reflected on his tenure at Holt.

"I joined the company 10 years ago as a mid-level manager inspired by his leadership; he groomed me into the person I am today." Aldy's hands clasped together, a rare display of emotion. "It was a big responsibility to take over three years ago. I am still not sure if I am doing a good job of keeping up his legacy."

The room held its breath, the weight of his words pressing against the glass walls. Tony leaned forward, the light glinting off his polished cufflinks. His voice cut through the tension, affirming and clear.

"John did pick the right successor," Tony interjected with unwavering conviction. "He was smart about picking the right people." He locked eyes with Aldy, an unspoken solidarity passing between them. "He did see the potential in you to be the next leader as the CEO of Holt."

Tony then stood, hands resting on the table, as he looked around at their colleagues. "We've seen the results in the last three years." His voice grew animated as he spoke of

Aldy's accomplishments. "His leadership style—decisive, innovative—has driven growth for everyone."

The others in the room nodded, their expressions softening into agreement. Tony's words seemed to act as a catalyst, transforming Aldy's moment of self-doubt into a collective affirmation of his leadership.

"His track record speaks for itself," Tony continued, gesturing with an open hand towards Aldy. "Delivering complex, high-level initiatives isn't just about crossing off objectives; it's about vision and follow-through. And that's exactly what Aldy brings to the table."

Audrey chimed in from her seat by the window, her voice smooth and reassuring. "Our market share has expanded significantly under your direction, Aldy." She paused for emphasis. "That's not coincidence—it's leadership."

Christina nodded along with Audrey's words, her eyes reflecting pride in their shared accomplishments.

Anto chimed in last but firmly from his corner of the room. "Our innovation pipeline is stronger than ever," he said with a slight smile playing on his lips.

The room pulsed with a renewed sense of purpose as Aldy absorbed their collective confidence. It bolstered him more than any financial report ever could—the unwavering support of his team.

***

The conference room's atmosphere grew dense with Anto's authoritative voice as she commandeered the discussion. Charts and graphs adorned the walls, reflecting Holt's steady financial trajectory. "We're on target," she began, her tone steady as a drumbeat. "Our numbers align with projections, and our performance matches industry standards."

Around the table, heads nodded in agreement. The facts were clear: Holt was holding its own in a turbulent market.

Aldy's chair creaked as he leaned forward, his eyes piercing the veil of complacency. "So what's our next chapter?" he challenged. "Where's the growth that once defined us?"

Anto, unflustered, offered a slice of reality. "That's what's happening in the market," she said, fingers tapping a rhythm on the polished table. "Everyone is growing at the same pace." A brief pause allowed her words to settle. "Some of our competitors are even struggling."

She reminded them that Holt's growth, although not stellar, was on par with its competition; no alarms were sounding.

"The board is neutral," Anto continued, her voice smooth as silk. "They are neither excited nor worried. They aren't pushing for change."

Aldy stood abruptly, his silhouette casting a long shadow across the room. "That's what worries me." His words sliced through the air like a cold breeze. "Why is no one seeing the trend? If we keep pace like this, we could be in trouble in a few years."

His gaze swept across the faces before him, each etched with varying degrees of concern and complacency. Aldy knew that survival in this industry didn't come from meeting expectations—it came from shattering them.

Audrey leaned back in her chair, the leather creaking softly under her weight, and steepled her fingers before her. Her gaze drifted across the polished surface of the conference table, reflecting the serious faces of her colleagues.

"You all know I'm not one for beating around the bush," she began, her voice carrying a certainty that drew everyone's attention. "Our clients—they've been with us for ages, and they're comfortable. But that comfort's a double-edged sword."

She paused, letting the words sink in. Anto nodded slightly, acknowledging the truth in her statement.

"They see us as reliable," Audrey continued. "But reliable's just another word for predictable these days. They don't just want us to support them; they're looking for us to guide them, to be their compass in this tech storm."

"A history of dependability has earned us their trust, no question," Audrey said, her tone sharpening to underscore her point. "Yet, trust alone won't secure our position at the forefront; it's the innovation that anticipates their needs, the foresight that sidesteps the pitfalls before they even come into view. They expect us to not only keep up with the waves of technological change but to harness those waves and chart a new path forward."

She let her gaze sweep the room, ensuring her message resonated with each of her colleagues. "Imagine our clients at the helm of a ship, steering through a maelstrom of tech advancements. They're not just seeking a safe harbor—they're searching for a navigator, someone with the vision to spot the winds of change and set the sails accordingly, exploiting those very gusts that would overwhelm the unprepared."

Audrey paused, leaning in. "We are that navigator," she declared. "But to lead, we must evolve our mindset. No longer is it enough to respond to calls for assistance. We must predict, vocalize, and block the threats the horizon conceals, all while highlighting the unprecedented opportunities that lie beyond. That's how we reinforce our indispensability—not merely as a vendor but as their indispensable advisor, their avant-garde lighthouse in this tumultuous tech seascape."

The room remained silent, each member digesting Audrey's perspective. It was a reality they had all observed but seldom articulated with such clarity.

"And let's face it," she pressed on, "our new acquisitions? They're scarce. And when we do land a new fish, it's hardly ever because we've dazzled them with innovation or strategic prowess."

Her fingers tapped an impatient rhythm on the table as she locked eyes with Aldy. "We're not just sellers anymore; we're supposed to be seers—prophets of tech—charting the course for these companies who are too scared to navigate these waters without a beacon."

Aldy leaned forward, propping his elbows on the table and interlocking his fingers. The intensity in Audrey's voice matched the urgency he felt within himself.

"You're spot on, Audrey," he said, meeting her unflinching stare. "It's time we take the helm in this relationship with our clients. We've been coasting on familiar tides for too long."

The room seemed to hold its breath as Audrey's words hung in the air, challenging each member of Holt's leadership team to confront the stagnation threatening their future.

Anto leaned back in her chair, her gaze sweeping across the gleaming table that reflected the sobering figures displayed on the screen behind her. "Let's talk numbers, folks. Our revenue mix—now that's a concern. Seventy percent hinges on low-cost services, competitive reselling, and support projects. What this means is simple: we lose a client, it's not a nick on the surface; it's a gouge."

Anto cleared her throat, drawing back the attention of her colleagues. "To be blunt," she continued, tapping the clear glass surface of the tablet before her which displayed charts and graphs in stark detail, "too much of our income is tied up in areas that offer little differentiation from our competitors. It's low-margin work that can easily be undercut."

She let her words hang in the room for a moment, ensuring every face was locked onto hers. "Consider this," she said as she gestured toward the screen, "low-cost services are dime a dozen in the market. They're essential, sure, but if that's where the bulk of our revenue lies, it positions us in a precarious place. We're like a one-trick pony in a field full of stallions."

Anto's gaze was steely, her voice a mix of concern and challenge. "We already run a lean operation, but if we lose even a single major client reliant on those services, it doesn't just dent our profits; it tears through them. It's a deep gouge that can take us a perilous amount of time to recover from."

The nods around the table showed understanding—if not agreement—from her colleagues, but it was clear she had spelled out a harsh truth that they would all need to grapple with.

The room absorbed her words, the weight of reliance on such precarious income evident in the furrowed brows around her. Aldy nodded along, his expression mirroring the gravity of Anto's assessment.

"That's right," Aldy chimed in, his hands braced on the table as he leaned forward, engaging everyone present with a look of earnest intensity. "And let's not overlook the razor-thin profit margins we're playing with here. IT services, product reselling—it's like trying to stand out in a bazaar where everyone's shouting just as loud and selling the same spices. The competition's fierce, and it's only getting fiercer."

A pause lingered in the air, filled only by the soft hum of electronics—a stark contrast to the tension among Holt's leadership. The stark reality of their position settled over them like a fog, clouding their path forward with uncertainty yet underscoring the urgency for change.

Christina shifted in her chair, the weight of the meeting's revelations settling on her shoulders. She caught Aldy's eye; the silent exchange between them heavy with unspoken urgency. With a sigh, she leaned forward, hands clasped on the polished conference table.

"Holt's lagging behind," she began, her voice carrying the weight of hard truths. "Our clients look to us to guide their innovation, but how can we lead when we're barely keeping up ourselves?"

Christina paused, gathering her thoughts, before letting them flow with deliberate impact. "Part of our struggle lies within. Our engineers—they're the lifeblood of Holt's innovation, but we've hit a wall in skill development and learning."

She scanned the room, letting her gaze rest on each of her colleagues as she spoke. "We've had no significant investment in education or training for new technologies. The industry is advancing at a breakneck pace, and we're not giving our team the tools they need to keep up, let alone lead."

Aldy's eyes narrowed in acknowledgment, his usual energetic demeanor tempered by the weight of Christina's insights. "We used to be at the forefront, sending our engineers to conferences, workshops, investing in certifications and cutting-edge research," she added, her voice tinged with a mix of frustration and resolve.

"We've settled into a routine that's comfortable, but comfort doesn't breed innovation. Our engineers are capable and intelligent, yet they're not challenged or motivated to push beyond the familiar. There's no incentive for them to experiment with new ideas or to take risks that could lead to breakthroughs."

Tony shifted in his chair, clearly uncomfortable but unable to refute the truth in Christina's words. "The potential is there, but without the opportunity and support to grow professionally, we're stifling their creativity. We're asking them to innovate without giving them the wings to fly."

Christina let her statement linger for a moment before concluding. "If we want to guide our clients' innovation, we first need to reignite the passion for learning and exploration within our own walls. Only then can we truly lead by example."

Around the table, brows furrowed, heads nodded in agreement. The sleek walls of the conference room seemed to close in, a stark reminder of the stifling status quo they found themselves trapped in.

"We're stretched thin," Christina continued. "Our margins are a joke, and because of that, we can't pour resources into new tech. We're running a race with weights on our ankles."

Aldy rested his chin on his steepled fingers, absorbing her words. Christina's gaze swept across her colleagues, each face reflecting the concern that gnawed at her.

"We need to refocus," she said, her tone firm. "It's not just about keeping the lights on anymore. It's about being a beacon for our clients, showing them what's possible."

The room fell silent for a moment, as if allowing Christina's words to echo and resonate with each person present. The truth was stark and undeniable: without innovation, Holt risked becoming obsolete in a world that waited for no one.

* * *

The conference room's tension had seeped into every corner, leaving a palpable silence hanging in the air after Christina's words. Tony, seated at the far end of the polished mahogany table, leaned forward. His fingers steepled, eyes scanning the faces of his colleagues. The gravity of their predicament weighed on him, and he recognized the necessity to add a critical dimension to their discussion.

"Hold up, folks," Tony interjected, breaking the contemplative stillness. "We're missin' a key piece here. It ain't just about innovation or profit margins."

The heads around the table turned toward him, faces etched with concern and curiosity.

"Our people," he continued, "the bloodline of Holt, they're starvin' for growth. Not just business growth—personal, professional development. We've been so tunnel-visioned on project work that we've neglected to offer 'em new learning opportunities."

Audrey nodded, her eyes reflecting acknowledgment of an overlooked truth.

Tony pushed back his chair and stood up, hands braced on the table. "Think about it—our top talent's walking out the door 'cause we're not feedin' their hunger to learn new tech. They're out there changin' the world while we're playin' catch-up."

Christina crossed her arms, considering his point. "He's right," she admitted softly.

"And it ain't just retention," Tony pressed on, walking slowly around the room, his hands gesturing emphatically as he spoke. "Attracting new blood? Good luck with that when word gets out that Holt's laggin' behind on cutting-edge work."

Tony halted near the gleaming whiteboard, dotted with the remnants of strategies past, and let his gaze sweep back over the room, locking eyes with each of his colleagues as if to draw them into his conviction. "Folks, we gotta face the hard truth. Our culture? It's stale. And in this valley, 'stale' might as well be the kiss of death," Tony asserted, his voice a blend of frustration and passion.

Heads around the table nodded, some with reluctance, as the gravity of his words set in. "See, the brightest minds out there, they're not just lookin' for a paycheck. They're huntin' for a frontier—a place to test their mettle and grow. Our competitors offer that in spades. What do we offer?" Tony's rhetorical question lingered in the air, heavy with implication.

Christina piped up, her tone somber yet supportive, "He's got a point. We've become too comfortable with the status quo, and it's costin' us—not just in profits, but in potential."

Tony seized on the moment, his voice rising with the urgency of their circumstances. "We used to be pioneers, remember? But now, we've let the garden overgrow. Without pruning, without cultivation, talent withers... or worse, it seeks more fertile ground."

Aldy's furrowed brow showed his concern, recognizing the multifaceted problem they faced. "So, our image, it's...?"

"It's tarnished," Tony cut in, unafraid to state the uncomfortable truth. "Out there, in the market? Holt's seen as a dinosaur. And that image it's keepin' the new breed of tech innovators from even considerin' us. We've got to change not just the reality of what we offer, but perception too."

Aldy rubbed his chin thoughtfully. "You're sayin' our culture is pushing talent away?"

"Exactly," Tony affirmed with a sharp nod. "We've made it too easy for 'em to find better opportunities elsewhere."

Audrey leaned back in her chair, absorbing the picture Tony painted—a dire one, but not without hope. "We need to become a magnet for talent again; make it clear that Holt is where the future's being written."

Tony nodded fervently, driven by the belief that they were standing at a crossroads. "That's why we have to turn this ship around, starting with our very core. Our culture, our brand, everything." With a steady gaze, he concluded, "If we foster a culture that celebrates growth and innovation, we won't just retain our best—we'll attract the best. That's how we reclaim the edge that put us on the map in the first place."

Aldy leaned back in his chair, fingers steepled beneath his chin, as he absorbed the weight of his team's concerns. The conference room's glass walls echoed back their words, a stark reminder of the transparency he sought within Holt's culture. Each voice had woven a tapestry of challenges, from financial dependencies to a dire need for employee development.

He stood and paced to the window, gazing out at the Silicon Valley skyline. The sun dipped behind the buildings, casting long shadows that seemed to stretch across the city, like the growing competition threatening to overshadow Holt.

In the silence that followed Tony's call for an emphasis on professional growth, Aldy felt the pieces click into place. They had become too comfortable and familiar with their current pace. Their rivals weren't just matching strides; they were sprinting ahead. Aldy knew it was time for a seismic shift—a fundamental change that would rattle the very foundations of Holt and propel them forward.

He turned to face his colleagues, their faces a mosaic of anticipation and uncertainty. "We've built something great here," he began, his voice steady and resolute.

"But greatness isn't a plateau; it's a peak we have to climb over and over again."

Aldy walked slowly around the table, locking eyes with each member of his team. "Holt needs more than just incremental improvements; we need a vision so bold it'll carve out new markets and redefine our role in this industry."

Audrey nodded, her expression reflecting a mixture of excitement and apprehension. Anto jotted down notes, his brow furrowed in concentration. Christina leaned forward, her eyes alight with the spark of challenge.

"We can't wait for someone else to ask us to change," Aldy continued. "We need to be the ones who leap before being pushed. The next board meeting is our chance to lay out this new vision—a plan that will not only secure our growth but will ensure Holt remains synonymous with innovation."

His declaration hung in the air like a challenge to fate itself.

Aldy could feel the energy shift in the room, as if his words had breathed life into dormant ambitions. His team exchanged glances, silent conversations passing between them as they contemplated the enormity of what lay ahead.

The sun had vanished now, leaving behind only its afterglow, that lingered like a promise on the horizon. In that moment of twilight clarity, Aldy understood that complacency was their greatest adversary, and it was one they could no longer afford to entertain.

As he gathered his notes and prepared to adjourn the meeting, Aldy knew what needed to be done. He would craft a plan audacious enough to stir the board into action—a strategy that would anchor Holt's future firmly in innovation.

With resolve etched into every line of his face, Aldy offered his team a final nod. "Let's get ready to shake things up," he said with a smile that held more determination than warmth.

The chapter closed on a company at the cusp of transformation, led by a CEO who saw beyond current success to potential greatness—Aldy, with his heart set on revolutionizing Holt from within.

A BRIGHT IDEA
MAPPING UNCHARTED TERRITORY

In the soft glow of predawn light, the usually bustling Silicon Valley headquarters of Holt found its rhythm temporarily stilled. As the first rays of the morning sun began to kiss the skyline, Aldy stood contemplatively at his office window, overlooking the garden courtyard. The calm before the storm of innovation and enterprise marked the start of another feverish day.

Abruptly, he turned on his heel, his resolve solidifying with each step toward his desk. With a swift motion, he sent a text to his leadership team: "Emergency meeting—my office, ASAP. It's time we strategize our next move." In minutes, the stillness of the early hour was displaced by a sense of urgency.

Tony, still with his jacket over his arm and coffee in hand, was the first to arrive. Aldy nodded briskly in acknowledgment as he gestured to the couch area, where an informal circle of chairs awaited them.

"I appreciate the early call, Aldy," Tony said, setting his coffee aside. "What's the play?"

"We're plotting our future. Time to pivot, and fast," Aldy replied with a decisive tone, the glint of the dawning day reflecting in his eyes.

Audrey swept into the room just as the last stars retreated from the morning sky. Her brisk pace and an expression of focused curiosity bespoke her readiness to tackle whatever challenge lay before them.

Aldy greeted her with a nod of respect. "Audrey, good, you're here. We need to reassess today."

The trio huddled together, the room abuzz with hushed voices and the occasional rustle of papers, as they started to lay the groundwork for a bold new chapter. The impromptu gathering, absent of formal agendas and projected presentations, created an atmosphere charged with potential and an implicit understanding that from this meeting, a new course would be charted, one that could reshape Holt's destiny.

Aldy leaned back in his chair, fingers steepled before him, his gaze sharp. "We can't keep circling the same old ideas, expecting a breakthrough. It's time we cast a wider net—learn from the trailblazers."

Audrey nodded, her expression a blend of contemplation and resolve. "There's a cloud technology conference in Vegas soon. It's a melting pot of innovation and experience—it might just be what we need."

Tony leaned forward, resting his elbows on the desk. "The who's who of tech will be there. If there are new strategies out there working wonders, that's where we'll find them."

Officially titled "CloudNext," this marquee event draws over 20,000 attendees every year to glimpse the future of cloud computing. The four-day agenda overflows with 400+ sessions led by renowned experts across technologies like AI, blockchain, quantum computing, and more.

But CloudNext's main lure is unparalleled access to pioneering case studies from enterprises that leveraged the cloud to transform. The keynote stage attracts famous Fortune 500 CEOs and unicorn founders to share their digital innovation successes.

This year also features an immersive exhibit floor with interactive demos from 1,000+ cloud-based startups. The entire ecosystem promotes invaluable cross-pollination of ideas between market leaders.

Attending CloudNext aligns perfectly with Holt's imperative to rapidly adapt in order to compete. Surrounded by bleeding-edge innovations, Holt can scout the latest cloud-enabled capabilities to build customer solutions. They can also discover new monetization models, partnership strategies, and skills development required on this journey."

Aldy leaned forward, intrigued by the idea. "That sounds promising. Let's look at the agenda." As Audrey pulled up the CloudNext agenda, the team's excitement grew palpable. The 4-day schedule overflowed with insights across 400+ sessions, promising immense wisdom.

They poured over the conference agenda on a tablet, scrolling through keynotes and breakout sessions. Topics ranged from leveraging artificial intelligence in cloud solutions to implementing next-generation cybersecurity.

"This one," Aldy said, tapping the screen, where a panel discussion on emerging market trends was listed. "If we can get ahead of these curves..."

Audrey pointed to another session focused on strategic partnerships and cross-industry collaborations. "Here too. We need to broaden our horizons—see beyond just our slice of the pie."

Equally compelling were the customer keynotes from enterprises that created a competitive advantage using the latest technologies. A UPS VP would detail their business transformation journey leveraging technology. Disney's CIO presented on creating new business models that helped them generate new revenue streams. These inspiring case studies aligned smoothly with Holt's own goals.

As they perused the conference details, it became clear that this event would provide a wealth of knowledge and inspiration for Holt's leadership team. They decided to attend the conference together, and Tony offered his support.

Aldy decided the entire 8-member leadership contingent must attend to absorb these exponential visions. He asked his executive assistant Emma to handle the travel logistics for what he cheekily dubbed "Cloud Camp.".

Emma quickly booked out a compact wing of suites at Aria Resort, conveniently located alongside the CloudNext venue. She also coordinated flights and planned transportation, plus evening group dinners to discuss key takeaways.

"We're not just going to sit back and watch," Aldy said as they concluded their plans. "We're stepping into the ring with these giants."

With an itinerary set and anticipation brewing like an electric current between them, they dispersed from Aldy's office with a newfound sense of purpose. Tony offered a parting thought before slipping out the door.

"We're not just learning; we're scouting for allies. Let's remember that."

Aldy watched his team depart, feeling the weight of expectation lift ever so slightly. The upcoming conference was more than an opportunity—it was a call to arms for Holt to reclaim its place at the forefront of technological evolution.

***

The lights of Las Vegas glittered like a galaxy spilled across the desert floor as Aldy and his team descended from the plane. Their eyes flickered with reflections of neon, a silent testament to the city that never slept. The technical architects from Christina's team, minds brimming with codes and algorithms, clustered around their director, ready for the mission ahead.

In the lobby of their chosen hotel, a glass and steel monument to modernity, Tony leaned against the check-in counter. He flipped open his sleek planner, his gaze piercing through the throng of tourists and gamblers.

"We split up," he suggested, voice firm over the din of slot machines. "Business on one side, tech on the other. We need to cover more ground."

Audrey nodded, strands of her hair catching light from the chandeliers above. "Smart. We'll absorb more that way."

Christina produced a tablet from her bag, her fingers dancing across the screen with practiced ease. "I've mapped out the sessions," she said, eyes focused as she swiped through a color-coded schedule. "These are the must-attends for each group."

The technical architects gathered around her, heads tilting to catch glimpses of their week laid out in pixels and taps.

Aldy surveyed his team—faces set with purpose amidst the buzz of Vegas—and felt a surge of pride. This was his crew, his champions in the field of innovation.

"Alright," he said with a grin that held promise. "Let's conquer this conference."

They split into their groups with a sense of camaraderie only found in those about to embark on an adventure together. The business-focused contingent followed Audrey's confident strides towards sessions on market trends and strategic partnerships. Meanwhile, Tony led his contingent of tech gurus toward workshops promising insights into cloud technologies and AI advancements.

Christina stayed central to both groups, bridging them with her analytical mind and keen sense of organization. She would be their lynchpin as they navigated through the maze of knowledge that awaited them.

As night fell over Las Vegas, the team retired to their rooms, each person laying out business cards like battle plans for the days ahead. They knew when they reconvened at week's end, they would be armed with fresh ideas and potential alliances.

In his room overlooking the Strip, Aldy stood at the window, watching the ceaseless dance of lights below.

Tomorrow they would dive into a sea of possibility—and he was ready to swim against any current to bring Holt back to its rightful place at the forefront of technology services.

***

Morning light filtered through the vast windows of the hotel's breakfast area, casting a warm glow on the tables. Aldy, Audrey, and Tony sat at a corner table, each nursing a cup of coffee as they reviewed the day's agenda. The buzz of conversation around them ebbed and flowed like a living thing, with occasional bursts of laughter punctuating the air.

Audrey flipped through her conference app, scrolling past various sessions and workshops. "This keynote is a big deal," she remarked, her eyes not leaving the screen. "People have been talking about it since we landed."

Tony leaned back in his chair, arms crossed. "They're expecting revelations—trends, new services, maybe even strategic partnerships. Could be a goldmine for us if we play our cards right."

Aldy sipped his coffee thoughtfully. Around them, clusters of attendees from all over the globe chatted animatedly about the day ahead. He could sense the undercurrent of excitement—a collective eagerness to glimpse into the future of cloud technology.

"What's got everyone so wound up?" Aldy mused aloud. "It's not just another product launch or service update. There's something more."

Audrey looked up from her conference itinerary, dotted with her neat annotations about each event, and met Aldy's contemplative gaze. "You're right about that," she began, her voice carrying a weight of intrigue. "Word on the street is that this year's keynote is set to unveil something big—a game changer, as some have called it. And if the whispers I've heard are even half true, we might be looking at a major shift in the cloud computing landscape."

She took a moment to ensure she had Aldy's full attention before continuing. "Last year, the same keynote unexpectedly revealed that self-optimizing cloud infrastructure, remember? It was a jaw-dropper. We gave everyone a run for their money, and honestly, we hadn't seen it coming. This type of innovation is precisely what keeps the industry on its toes, and they're good at it."

Aldy leaned in, intrigued. "So what's the buzz about this year?"

"It's all very hush-hush, but from following their movements, their acquisitions, and their recent hires, I'd say they're expanding beyond simple cloud services. They're aiming to integrate AI systems in a way we haven't seen before. Think massive data handling with real-time, adaptive learning capabilities. They're pushing the envelope—again."

Audrey's eyes shone with a hint of admiration and competitive fire. "We need to be prepared for whatever it is. It's not just another run-of-the-mill update; this could very well redefine how businesses interact with the cloud. We need to watch closely and learn as much as we can. It's exactly the innovative leap we've been talking about—if they pull it off, it could leave a lot of players, including us, playing catch-up."

The possibility sparked a fresh sense of urgency in Aldy. He realized that this conference wasn't just an opportunity for networking and ideas—it could be the very place they witness the next leap in their industry.

A server approached, refilling their cups with a practiced smile before gliding away to attend to other guests.

Tony drummed his fingers on the table. "We've spoken with folks from startups to behemoths these past two days," he said. "They all circle back to this keynote like it's a beacon."

Aldy leaned forward, resting his elbows on the table. The early hour had done nothing to dull his sharp focus; if anything, it sharpened his resolve.

"We need to listen closely," Aldy said decisively. "There might be an opportunity for Holt here—an alliance or an insight that could redefine our trajectory."

The clink of cutlery and murmur of voices surrounded them as they planned their approach to the keynote session. The air was thick with anticipation and the rich aroma of coffee.

As they rose from their seats to join the stream of professionals heading toward the conference hall, Aldy felt a spark ignite within him. The prospect of discovery filled him with an energy that mirrored the vibrant city outside. Whatever secrets awaited in that keynote address could very well be the catalyst Holt needed to soar anew.

***

Aldy settled into his seat, the soft hum of conversation around him fading as the lights dimmed. The massive screen at the front of the conference hall flickered to life, and with it, the future of technology began to unfold. He leaned forward, elbows on knees, eyes locked on the images and words cascading before him.

One after another, industry leaders took the stage. Each presentation introduced new products and services that seemed to leap from the realms of science fiction into stark reality. Customers shared their success stories—tales of transformation and triumph through technology. They spoke not only of supporting their business with these advancements but of being wholly reborn because of them.

Aldy watched as a healthcare giant showcased an AI-driven diagnostic system, that could predict patient outcomes with startling accuracy. A retail conglomerate demonstrated a virtual shopping assistant that personalized each customer's experience through machine learning. A finance firm revealed a blockchain-based transaction platform that promised unprecedented security and speed.

With each revelation, Aldy felt a jolt—a spark igniting within him. Technology was no longer a mere scaffold; it had become the keystone. Large enterprises were morphing into powerhouses that delivered business solutions anchored in technological ingenuity. These were not mere changes; they were revolutions.

He noticed consumers' behaviors on screen—interacting with smart devices as if they were extensions of their own bodies, making decisions based on predictive analytics, and forming new social patterns woven by digital threads. Technology had infiltrated every aspect of life, reshaping how humans connected and thrived.

Aldy's thoughts raced as he scribbled notes feverishly. Each company on stage was not only adapting to new technologies; they were actively shaping them, pushing boundaries to create what didn't exist before. Innovation wasn't an afterthought—it was their heartbeat.

As he absorbed these insights, Aldy's vision for Holt crystallized. It wasn't enough to walk alongside these giants; Holt had to join their ranks to become a leader in harnessing technology's raw potential to drive business forward.

He exchanged glances with Audrey and Tony as another speaker detailed their company's roadmap for the next decade—a canvas painted with bold strokes of innovation and daring dreams.

They understood then that Holt's transformation was inevitable—and essential. It was time for Aldy to weave these patterns into a new tapestry for Holt, one that would place them at the vanguard of technological evolution.

Aldy navigated the crowded conference floor with an analytical eye, weaving through a labyrinth of cutting-edge exhibits and eager representatives. His mind raced, tallying the plethora of services showcased: cybersecurity measures, cloud infrastructure management, bespoke software development—each company presenting its answer to the modern enterprise's prayers.

As he absorbed the energy around him, he couldn't shake the realization that these enterprise customers represented untapped potential for Holt. They possessed ambitious visions for digital transformation but lacked the strategic partnerships necessary to make those visions a reality. It was an opportunity ripe for the taking.

Aldy paused by a sleek booth, where a demo on predictive analytics caught his attention. The company behind it boasted an impressive client list; they didn't just sell software—they sold foresight. A few steps further, another exhibitor explained how their integrated IoT solutions transformed data into actionable intelligence for their clients.

It dawned on Aldy that Holt's role in this ecosystem wasn't just to provide a service—it was to craft an outcome. The key lay in understanding these enterprises' core challenges and offering not just technology but holistic business solutions.

As he continued his reconnaissance, he overheard snippets of conversation about partnerships and long-term engagements. The competitors didn't just offer piecemeal fixes; they provided comprehensive strategies that carried businesses into the future.

A spark ignited within Aldy's thoughts. To thrive, Holt needed to transcend the image of a vendor and become a visionary ally. He envisioned Holt devising platforms that married business acumen with technical innovation—platforms that could revolutionize how their clients operated and engaged with their own customers.

The concept crystallized in Aldy's mind: Holt would cultivate partnerships by selling business and technology solutions tailored to propel enterprises toward their ambitious goals. It was what the market demanded from its leaders and what it rewarded.

He made his way back to his team, excitement bubbling under his composed exterior. He had found the missing piece of the puzzle—the direction that would redefine Holt's identity and ensure its growth as a strategic partner in an ever-evolving technological landscape.

***

Under the luminescent glow of the Las Vegas skyline, Aldy, Audrey, and Tony found themselves at a round table in a bustling restaurant, plates of half-eaten food pushed aside as their conversation took center stage. The clink of silverware and low hum of conversations around them provided a backdrop to their intense discussion.

"That keynote," Aldy began, his eyes wide with the fire of realization, "did you catch how Allen from Optix AI just... commanded the room?"

Audrey nodded, her fork pausing mid-air. "Hard to miss. The guy's company shot up to a billion in valuation in no time flat. It's like they're riding the tech wave on a rocket."

Tony leaned back, fingers drumming on the table. "It's their approach—providing end-to-end solutions. That's where they're winning."

Aldy's gaze sharpened, the cogs in his mind visibly turning. "Exactly! That's the opportunity staring us right in the face." He leaned forward, elbows on the table, lowering his voice as if sharing a coveted secret. "Optix isn't just selling products; they're selling outcomes and experiences. That's where we pivot."

Audrey chewed thoughtfully, considering Aldy's words. "So you're saying Holt should morph into... what? A solutions architect?"

"More than that," Aldy countered with fervor. "We need to be their compass in this digital jungle—navigate them through transformation, not just sell them tools for it."

Tony nodded slowly, absorbing the shift in perspective. "Makes sense. But we're only scratching the surface of what Optix is doing."

Aldy straightened up as a plan began to form. "We need to dive deeper—understand their strategies, dissect their success."

Audrey wiped her mouth with a napkin and tossed it onto her plate decisively. "I'm game. We reach out to Allen then? Pick his brain on how Optix is crafting these solutions?"

"That's our next move," Aldy confirmed with an approving nod.

The trio exchanged glances that spoke volumes—a silent pact forming between them as they recognized the potential for change within their grasp.

Tony picked up his phone, already drafting an email in his mind. "I'll reach out to Allen's team today—see if we can set up a deep dive session with him."

Aldy leaned back in satisfaction as Audrey offered a rare smile of agreement. Their agenda was clear now; they were on a quest for knowledge—to transform not just Holt but their own understanding of what it meant to be leaders in technology.

As they exited the restaurant, stepping back into the pulsating heart of Las Vegas, Aldy couldn't help but feel that this was more than just another conference detour—it was the beginning of Holt's rebirth into something greater, something formidable.

With a newfound solidarity permeating their stride, they advanced into an afternoon that had shifted its complexion, now painted with intention and potential—a future where Holt would not merely follow in the footsteps of others but carve out new pathways with inventive ideas and strategic alliances.

RISE OF SOLUTIONS

THE NEW CURRENCY OF VALUE CREATION

T he sun dipped below the horizon, casting an amber glow over the bustling streets of Las Vegas. Inside the conference center, Aldy and his team traversed from one session to another, soaking in tales of technological metamorphoses that reshaped companies far and wide. As dusk settled and neon lights flickered to life, they amassed a wealth of knowledge on solution selling—a beacon for Holt's future.

As the day's final session concluded, Aldy strode through the crowd, his mind teeming with ideas. It was then that he spotted Mark emerging from the throng. With a firm handshake and a shared nod toward innovation, Aldy extended an invitation to dinner. The popular steakhouse buzzed with the energy of satisfied patrons when they arrived.

Around the elegant table, silverware glinted under soft lighting as Aldy, Audrey, and Mark exchanged impressions of the day's revelations. Upon hearing Aldy articulate the potential of solution selling, a vibrant spark ignited within Mark's gaze. He sprang to his feet, his fervor rippling through the air and drawing a tapestry of curious glances from around the room.

"Solutions!" Mark's voice crescendoed, his hands carving emphatic arcs before him. "That's exactly what we're starved for at Doll Inc.—a dire shortage of progressive ideas."

Aldy: "So, Mark, level with me. Where's the bottleneck at Doll Inc. holding back change?"

Mark sighs, swirling his bourbon

Mark: "Truthfully, Aldy? Our customer service strategy feels trapped in the stone age. Scripts are so rigid, they drive folks mad rather than solve problems."

He shakes his head bitterly

"Meanwhile our competitors implement AI, predictive tech, full revolution of support,. Yet our leadership clings to the past, lacking any vision to drive innovation."

Mark takes a long drag of his drink

"I've begged them to modernize, shift from break-fix transactions to proactive advice. But between obstinate legacy execs, and now revenue concerns limiting risk, I bang my head daily against hardened walls."

Mark looks pleadingly at Aldy

"I can't transform this old battleship alone. The fear of disappointing customers haunts me daily. I desperately need strategic partners to spark ideas before our service loyalty completely erodes. Tell me, how do we ignite innovation in this stubborn relic?!"

Mark swirls the bourbon in his glass, gazing thoughtfully

Mark: "Y'know Aldy, I'm tired of solution providers limiting imagination with 'what do you need' drudgery."

He leans back, gesturing in the air

"We should be indulging in a sumptuous feast of possibilities! Proactive brainstorming unconstrained by convention."

Mark meets Aldy's curious eyes

"I want to explore the art of the possible with innovators like yourself. Wow me with the essence of cutting-edge capabilities made tangible. Illuminate new frontiers beyond my visibility."

His voice grows fervent, fist clenched in determination

"Revolutionize my concept of customer service! Make me believe we can traverse galaxies beyond my static constellations. Seed my mind and watch disruptive ideas flourish!"

Mark's zeal fills their conversation, fueling his vision for transformation

"In short, don't ask me what Doll Inc. needs; reveal to me what Holt can envision our future to be!"

Mark's animated proclamation reverberated through the upscale eatery, his animated gestures underscoring his speech. Patrons turned, their chatter fading into silence, captivated as Mark's voice grew. The establishment's polished wood, glinting silverware, and soft candle glow appeared to still, attentive to a momentous revelation.

Audrey leaned forward, her voice tinged with persuasive zest. "We can bridge that gap for you. Holt has the talent pool ready to dive into any challenge."

Aldy observed Mark's reaction, noting the slight shift in his posture—an indication of skepticism or perhaps a desire for more than just an eager sales pitch. He steered the conversation towards collaboration.

"Right," Aldy chimed in smoothly, "the key lies in crafting solutions that resonate with your needs without overburdening your team."

Mark settled back into his seat, nodding. "Your support has been stellar over these years," he said warmly. "I'm rooting for Holt's success, and I'm here to back you up."

The rest of the evening unwound like a spool of silk—smooth and engaging—with ideas exchanged over succulent steaks and rich wine. Laughter peppered their strategic discourse as possibilities blossomed like desert flowers after rain.

As they stood to leave, an unspoken consensus hummed between them: this dinner marked not just the end of a day but also the dawn of thrilling prospects. With each handshake and parting smile, anticipation for what lay ahead charged the air like static before a storm.

Outside, the Las Vegas skyline twinkled against the night sky—a canopy of stars mirrored by man-made constellations—as Aldy and his companions dispersed into the neon embrace, their minds alight with thoughts and excitement for a transformed future.

***

The morning air hummed with potential as Aldy and Audrey converged outside the coffee shop, the aroma of freshly brewed beans swirling around them. With the rush of the day ahead, they forwent a sit-down breakfast for the swift grab-and-go of steaming cups.

Audrey approached, her heels announcing her arrival with sharp staccato clips against the marble. In her tailored suit and sleek updo, she cut a striking pose, but her smile seemed strained.

"No time for breakfast either, huh?" She greeted Aldy, gesturing at the coffee cup doubling as his meal.

"I'm going to find sessions to learn more about solutions," Aldy declared, his voice a mix of determination and caffeine-fueled urgency. He flipped open his laptop, fingers dancing across the keyboard, eyes scanning the conference schedule with a predator's precision.

He glanced up briefly. "I'm cramming my schedule with as many solution-focused sessions as I can. We only have a few days here to soak up everything we can." His words tumbled out rapidly, keeping pace with his browsing.

Audrey nodded, cradling her own cup, steam fogging her glasses momentarily. "I'll do the same from a sales angle." She was cautious, unwilling to leap without looking. "But I need to make sure we're not chasing after some new buzzword or ephemeral trend."

"Absolutely," Aldy agreed, his gaze never leaving the screen as he continued to register for sessions. "Try to learn as much as you can. Let's sync up later and compare notes."

Audrey perceived Aldy's eagerness to disengage from their conversation—his focus already shifting towards the plethora of sessions beckoning him. The anticipation in his posture was palpable, like a runner at the starting blocks.

"I'm going to run to this session that starts in three minutes," Aldy blurted out suddenly, glancing at his watch—a sleek piece that mirrored his swift lifestyle. "I'm almost late." His words tumbled out in haste.

With that brief farewell hanging in the air, Aldy took off, weaving through the crowd with an athlete's agility. "I'll see you later!" he called over his shoulder, his figure rapidly becoming one with the sea of conference attendees.

Audrey watched him disappear into the throng, her own mind already cataloging which sales sessions would yield the most valuable insights. With a last sip of her coffee that burnt just slightly against her lips, she squared her shoulders and headed towards her first session of the day.

Aldy slid into the back row of the conference room, a well-manicured skepticism furrowing his brow. The session title loomed on the screen in bold: "Revolutionizing Retail: Next-Gen Supply Chain Solutions." The cogs of his mind churned with a thread of conceit. These strategies, these technologies, they were familiar territories, pages from an old playbook. He pondered, anticipation tinged with skepticism, what groundbreaking innovation could possibly be waiting in the wings?

The presenter, a woman named Mary with an air of unassuming expertise, stepped to the podium. Her opening remarks cut through Aldy's cynicism, anchoring the discussion in real-world challenges that retailers faced—issues that were invisible yet crippling to their operations.

Aldy watched as real-world examples brought the issue into sharp focus, revealing systemic blind spots wrestling with uncertainty. He saw heat maps of risk pulsating through global shipping channels and demand signals lost in delays and distortions.

Aldy leaned forward, interest piqued as she narrated tales of transformation, businesses that had been blind to their own inefficiencies now thriving with newfound clarity and purpose. He could almost hear the cash registers ringing in harmony with her every word.

She then peeled back the layers of technology like an expert chef revealing the secrets to a complex dish. Each ingredient—a sprinkle of AI here, a dash of blockchain there—was chosen not just for its flavor but for its ability to blend seamlessly into the existing enterprise palate.

"Much of this turbulence is inevitable in complex retail ecosystems," the presenter continued. "But what if technology could illuminate the unknowns? Reveal interdependencies invisible to human eyes?"

As a solution took shape combining predictive analytics, automation, and warehouse robots churning a symphony of data into decision intelligence, Aldy witnessed an elegant response to volatility. More strikingly, he saw the presenter contextualizing technology within broader business outcomes—stabilizing supply chains to unlock revenue and fortify customer loyalty.

Aldy's pulse quickened when integration became the focal point. The woman spoke of adaptability not as an afterthought but as a keystone—melding new tech with old, meshing silicon with human sinew, intertwining process with practice.

The presentation concluded with a demo of existing integration, accelerating deployment. As Aldy watched legacy infrastructure seamlessly ingest bleeding-edge algorithms, the lightning bolt struck—their technology partners excel at building tools but stumble at driving adoption. This solution consolidated both, undoubtedly rocketing ROI.

Our partners hawk their wares well enough, he mused, but they falter at the human hurdle. Adoption—a beast they barely tame.

Aldy's realization illuminated the stumbling block shared by Holt's tech part-ners—they were craftsmen in a silo, adept at creating robust tools yet lacking the finesse to paint them into the broader canvas of their clients' operations. As the session continued to unfold, Aldy's insights deepened, shaping the contours of a challenge Holt could rise to meet.

Business Insight: The tech partners were maestros of their craft but tone-deaf to the symphony of business needs. They understood their instruments—algorithms, data pipelines, sensor networks—but not the music they needed to play. They sold solutions in a vacuum, ignoring how those solutions should resonate with the business strategies, priorities, and market pressures each unique enterprise faced. Aldy sketched the outlines of Holt's edge—to not only deliver tools but to read the unwritten verses of their clients' corporate narratives, translating challenges into finely tuned strategies enabled by tech.

Cutting-Edge Technology: Indisputably, the partners were on the bleeding edge, but bleeding-edge can be a double-edged sword when tech sophistication eclipses utility. They pitched marvels of engineering that promised to usher in tomorrow's era today, yet the marvels often sat on shelves gathering dust. Aldy knew Holt had to bridge the gap—innovation was only as valuable as its applicability. He envisioned Holt crafting not just the tools of the future but the keys that unlocked the present potential of every client.

Seamless Integration: Integration was the partners' Achilles heel, the chink in their otherwise impenetrable armor. They could architect the future in theory but failed to graft it onto the lived reality of legacy systems and workflows. Their solutions were islands of potential disconnected from the mainland of daily operations. In Aldy's mind, a vision of Holt's way forward took shape—becoming the bridge builders who could integrate the new world with the old, weaving innovation into the fabric of existing infrastructures without tearing seams or disrupting the patterns of work that kept businesses humming.

Aldy scribbled with an urgency fueled by inspiration. Uniting business insight, tech prowess, and integration meant Holt could not just peddle but implement change. Their offering would not be a product but a promise—handing over not a tool, but a turning point.

The realization dawned bright and sharp. If Holt could harness these three pillars—1. business insight, 2. cutting-edge tech, and 3. seamless integration—they could offer en-terprises more than just tools; they could deliver transformation on a silver platter.

He jotted down notes feverishly, already envisioning Holt's new mantra: Technology tailored for adoption—a no-brainer for any enterprise starved for change.

Aldy eased into a seat at the back of the AI-ML session, the words 'Gen AI' splashed in bold across the projector screen. He folded his arms, a half-smirk dancing on his lips. *Gen AI, just another gimmick to catch the eye,* he mused, but he was here now, might as well soak up what he could.

The room buzzed with the murmur of tech leaders and data scientists, a stark contrast to the business-centric crowd from the supply chain discussion. Aldy watched them, their gazes fixed on the presenter, their postures tense with anticipation. These were the folks in the trenches of technology, grappling with code and systems more than profit margins and market shares.

The presenter stepped up, her voice clear and assured, as she laid out the problem statement. Aldy's smirk faded as she wove vivid examples of inefficiencies in current tech infrastructures. The solutions she promised were not just improvements, but revolutions in operational workflow.

Aldy leaned forward. The case studies pointed to staggering reductions in manual labor hours and boosts in productivity. This wasn't about dazzling clients with shiny new business strategies; it was about empowering companies from within by streamlining their technological backbone.

He scribbled notes furiously, his mind racing. Holt had been preoccupied with market visibility and innovative products but neglected a crucial aspect: "operational excellenc e.". If they could harness this Gen AI to refine their internal operations, they'd not only cut costs but could pass those savings and efficiencies onto clients.

Aldy's pen flew over the pad, the brisk scritch-scratch of the ballpoint a testament to his frenetic thoughts. "Operational excellence," he repeated under his breath, the notion fervently embedding itself within his psyche. It dawned on him—Holt's preoccupation with innovation and flashy products might draw the eye, but without a streamlined core, they would always be building on an unstable foundation.

The presenter delved deeper, elucidating how integrating Gen AI across IT infrastructures could dramatically reshape business processes, transforming them from cumbersome, error-prone operations to models of precision and agility. She outlined scenarios where AI algorithms could preemptively solve IT issues before they became problems, predict needs for maintenance, and dynamically allocate resources where they were most needed, essentially allowing businesses to do more with less.

Aldy visualized his company employing these AI-driven tools to renovate not just their external offerings but their internal environment as well. He saw IT departments liberated from the quagmire of daily setbacks, their time freed to innovate rather than firefight.

"Imagine," the presenter said, her words like a beacon to Aldy, "a scenario where your IT isn't just a support service but a strategic business partner. Gen AI can provide insights from data it collects, makes recommendations, and even take actions based on predefined business goals and continuous learning."

Aldy considered how this shift could impact client relationships. With this technology, Holt wouldn't merely provide products; they would proffer a suite of IT solutions fostering operational efficiencies, minimizing downtime, and propelling business continuity. It was all about optimizing the engine that ran the vehicle of commerce, ensuring it purrs seamlessly, propelling the company toward uncharted business horizons. He envisioned proposing these concepts to clients, showing them clear pathways to boosting their profitability along with their productivity—making Holt an indispensable ally in their pursuit of business excellence.

His notes now read like a blueprint for a transformed corporate identity, a mesh of technology and strategy that could pivot Holt from a seller to an architect of operational renaissance. He glimpsed a future where every sale had an operational strategy tailpiece, a plan that could provide enduring value beyond the completion of a transaction.

As the crowd dispersed, Aldy lingered, his mind a whirlwind. He had come to the conference in search of innovation, but here, amidst the swirling potential of operational prowess, he found his true quarry. His determination solidified with purpose; this was the advent of a holistic Holt, a transformative leader poised to inaugurate a new era of tech-infused operational efficiency.

Aldy's skepticism waned as he envisioned a new facet to Holt's offerings: tech solutions that could revolutionize not just what companies did but how they did it. It was an untapped vein of gold in a mine that everyone had been walking past, looking for bigger, more obvious treasures.

As the session ended, Aldy remained seated, surrounded by a departing crowd. The puzzle pieces were falling into place—a strategy that combined both technology and business solutions, each enhancing the other's value. Holt could become a hybrid force in the industry, driving business forward with innovation while reinforcing it with solid technological efficiency.

He stood up slowly, ideas crystallizing with each step he took out of the conference room. There was much to do—research to conduct, plans to formulate—but Aldy felt a surge of excitement. This was what he had come for: not just to learn but to discover an opportunity that could redefine Holt's path forward.

Aldy's brow furrowed as he digested the words of the presenter, whose badge gleamed with the name 'Indu'. They had stepped into the corridor, a space where the hum of conversations from adjacent rooms created a backdrop to their own. His eyes narrowed, not in suspicion but in intense curiosity, a trait that had propelled him to the forefront of Holt's leadership.

"How does this differ from what we're doing at Holt to optimize customer technology?" Aldy asked, voice laced with genuine interest.

Indu nodded, her expression revealing an understanding of the weight behind his question. "The solutions we suggest are comprehensive," she began. "they're not just services; they're a full package. Think of it as the difference between providing ingredients and delivering a ready-to-bake meal."

She spoke of three pillars—1. business, 2. technology, and 3. integration—that encompassed people and processes. "A solution," Indu explained, "incorporates all these elements, along with best practices derived from experience. Many are prebuilt for easy configuration."

Aldy's mind raced. Prebuilt solutions meant scalability and agility—qualities he yearned for Holt to embody.

"You mean customers can avoid lengthy development cycles with these pre-configured solutions?" Aldy interjected.

"Exactly," Indu confirmed. "We don't have to reinvent the wheel every time they need a new technology solution."

As she detailed how software companies provided end-to-end solutions configured to specific needs, Aldy visualized a new horizon for Holt. The idea resonated within him; it was common sense, an evolution of the automation and reusability principles he had championed.

"If you take a full-stack website," Indu continued, her hands shaping the air as if crafting the very architecture she described, "instead of starting from zero for each client, we provide a foundational suite—the frontend, backend, and integration layers—all prebuilt."

Aldy's thoughts raced alongside Indu's words. This wasn't just about reducing development costs or speeding up time to market; it was about delivering precision-engineered solutions with minimal error.

Indu concluded with a flourish, "It's about delivering quality quickly and consistently."

The lightbulb moment was almost visible above Aldy's head as he connected the dots. Reusable building blocks for business—customizable yet robust—could revolutionize Holt's approach.

He offered Indu a smile that held both gratitude and newfound resolve. "Thank you," he said before they parted ways, each step back toward the conference room heavy with Aldy's burgeoning plans for transformation at Holt.

***

The sun dipped below the horizon, painting the sky in shades of burnt orange and twilight blue as the Holt team approached the venue for SalesX's happy hour. Neon signs flickered to life, and chatter spilled out from open doorways, a siren call to the night's potential.

Aldy stepped into the room, the hum of conversation wrapping around him like a familiar coat. The space thrummed with the energy of Silicon Valley's finest, each interaction a spark that could ignite new ideas or partnerships. His gaze swept over the crowd until it landed on Wilfred, SalesX's CEO, who commanded attention with an easy grace.

No sooner had Aldy entered than Wilfred caught sight of him. A seasoned navigator of these social shoals, Wilfred raised his hand in greeting, a beacon amidst the sea of faces.

"How's the evening treating you?" Wilfred asked as Aldy approached, his voice rich with experience and a hint of curiosity.

"Full of promise," Aldy replied, eyes alight with the fervor of his recent revelations. "Wilfred, I've been thinking—"

Without hesitation, Aldy launched into his epiphany on solutions-based selling. Words poured out like a dam breached, his passion undeniable.

Wilfred listened intently, nodding at intervals. "It's a crucial realization," he affirmed once Aldy paused for breath. "And about time you joined us in this thinking."

Just then, Audrey slipped into their circle. She offered a small nod to Wilfred before turning her attention to Aldy's animated expression.

"Have you considered how these innovative companies structure their pricing?" Wilfred steered the conversation toward a new horizon. "Outcome-based pricing is where it's at—customers can't resist investing in results."

Aldy hung on every word as if each were a thread leading him through a labyrinth. He had ventured deep into the maze but hadn't yet found this path.

"We've yet to delve into pricing strategies," Aldy admitted, his voice laced with a mixture of admiration and urgency. "It's clearly something we need to master."

Wilfred glanced over Aldy's shoulder and pointed out Allen mingling across the room. "Talk to Allen from Optix AI," he suggested with a conspiratorial smile. "He might just have the insights you're after."

Gratitude flickered across Aldy's face as he followed Wilfred's gesture toward Allen—a potential ally in their quest for transformation.

As they left the event, Audrey broke the silence between them. "Wilfred has a point," she said thoughtfully. "The sellers at these presentations seem to be thriving with solution sales."

"It's clear they're offering more than just products; they're selling a vision that aligns with customer needs. They're storytellers, crafting narratives that feature their solutions as the protagonist—a keys to unlocking potential in businesses."

She paused a moment, her gaze taking in the animated faces of the sales representatives around them, their expressions lit with the enthusiasm of successful connections made. "You see, it's not just about the tech," Audrey continued, "it's about understanding the client's challenges so intimately that the solution feels bespoke, like it was crafted just for them. That approach turns sales into partnerships, and price becomes a detail in the larger scheme of value."

Aldy listened intently, seeing the truth in her observation. Audrey was keenly aware of the evolving landscape, recognizing that these thriving salespeople had adapted to a consultative role, positioning themselves as essential aids in their customers' journey towards growth and innovation.

Aldy nodded, his mind racing ahead to their return home. "Let's map this out properly once we're back," he proposed with determination in his voice.

An agreement settled between them like an unspoken pact as they walked away from the restaurant into the evening air that buzzed with possibilities yet to be seized.

NEW KID ON THE BLOCK

OPTIX AI STORY

Aldy perched on the edge of his desk, his gaze fixed on the skyline stretching beyond his office window. Silicon Valley sprawled before him, a landscape of dreams forged in circuitry and code. A week had elapsed since the conference, yet his mind replayed the conversation with Allen, brief as it was—a dialogue that sparked a firestorm of thoughts.

The young CEO's words, while scarce, had unveiled a formula for growth that intrigued Aldy. Allen's company, Optix AI, surged ahead with youthful vigor and an appetite for learning. Aldy admired that—they were kindred spirits in that regard.

His fingers drummed on the polished surface of his desk. Optix's strategies—it was imperative to understand them. They could hold the key to vaulting Holt to new heights.

"Set up a meeting," Aldy had instructed his assistant upon returning from Vegas. The request bore fruit quicker than anticipated, and Allen was eager to meet again.

A winery nestled among rolling hills offered the perfect venue—an offsite sanctuary where business blended with leisure. Aldy imagined the rich aroma of aged oak barrels mingling with their strategic discourse.

He reached out to his team, extending an invitation to join him at the winery's private conference room. It promised an ambiance conducive to creativity and collaboration—qualities Holt needed in spades.

As he pondered their upcoming meeting, Aldy swiveled in his chair, turning his attention back inside. The office hummed with subdued energy—a hive of activity driven by a shared mission.

The meeting with Allen would be a vital step in shaping Holt's future. Aldy felt it in his bones—their conversation at the happy hour had been but a prelude to something greater.

His phone buzzed; a message from Audrey confirmed her attendance and her eagerness to explore Optix's strategies further. Tony and Christina chimed in shortly after, each conveying readiness to dive into the discussion with Allen.

Aldy leaned back, hands clasped behind his head, a smile tugging at his lips. This was more than a simple exchange of ideas; it was the beginning of transformation—a pivotal moment where old patterns would unravel and new ones would weave themselves into Holt's fabric.

With resolve firming his features, he stood up and strode toward the door. It was time to prepare for what lay ahead—a meeting that could very well redefine their approach to business and innovation.

The future beckoned with all its uncertainties and promises. And Aldy was ready to answer its call.

Vines curled around the trellis at the winery, their leaves whispering in the soft breeze as Allen arrived, the first to step onto the sun-drenched patio. His attire, a careful choice between casual and professional, clung to his frame—clearly a nod to the importance of this meeting. Optix AI, his brainchild, thrived but still paled beside Holt's vast empire. His fingers tapped a staccato rhythm on the folder he carried, betraying his eagerness.

Aldy watched Allen from the winery's entrance, his gaze narrowing slightly as he appraised the young CEO's attempt at formality. A well-prepared dossier on Optix AI lay in Aldy's mind, its contents ready to fuel their conversation. He approached with a handshake that bridged their worlds—innovation and enterprise meeting halfway.

"As I understand it," Aldy began, his voice carrying the weight of meticulous analysis, launching into a detailed exposition of his perception of Optix AI's core business model, illustrating his points with the precision often reserved for boardroom presentations.

Allen cut in with a wave of his hand and an easy smile. "Let me give you the rundown." He unfolded the story of Optix AI like a map to treasure. "My friend found himself engulfed in turmoil, wrestling with a defective AI chatbot that had caused a stir within the ranks of a Fortune 50 firm. Merely forty-eight hours after the issue came to my attention, I had devised an elegant solution that resolved the complexities seamlessly."

Allen's narrative continued seamlessly, elucidating the scalability of their solution. "After the initial success with the chatbot, we didn't just pat ourselves on the back. We saw the bigger picture."

He leaned in, sharing the inception of their broader strategy. "We refined the bot into a robust platform, addressing a variety of customer interactions. First, we developed user-friendly admin portals, enabling non-tech staff to manage access without any IT involvement. Then we enhanced our system for global expansion, integrating over twenty languages to serve international clients."

The Holt team hung on to every detail as Allen delineated further nuances. "Next, we linked AI dialogues with invaluable backend databases, such as CRMs and ticketing systems. This contextual adaptability allowed personalized conversations, tapping directly into customer histories."

Allen's eyes gleamed with the reflection of his vision as he continued. "But the real game-changer was our suite of off-the-shelf solutions. We identified industry-wide pinpoints—customer service deflection and boosting catalog search efficiencies."

The young CEO gestured as if painting a portrait of Optix AI's journey. "Imagine demo videos illustrating these solutions in action, outcomes like halving call volumes or multiplying search effectiveness tenfold."

A murmur of acknowledgment passed through Aldy and his team, recognition dawning upon them.

Audrey leaned forward, her sharp eyes reflecting interest and skepticism. "Scaling that quickly to numerous companies must've been complex."

Allen leaned back, his chair creaking under the weight of confidence. "It's straightforward when your product speaks for itself. Our sales team could clearly articulate the business impact and ROI. Offer a client a solution that pays for itself? It sells like wildfire."

The tailored demos spoke directly to the needs of their specific industries. And the solid ROI? Backed up by data from similar deployments."

Allen mimicked reeling in a fish, a simple gesture that encapsulated the sales closure. "No need for exhaustive scoping or bespoke pricing—in came fixed-fee bundles. The client's savings directed our revenue shares, making it a win-win."

"And you moved to revenue-based selling?" Audrey pressed.

Allen nodded. "Precisely. Invest a dollar, reap
two—it's simple math." He spread his hands wide
as if showing them the horizon line where business met innovation.

He paused, his narrative lingering in the air like the rich aroma of the surrounding
vineyard. "That strategy—turning innovation into a scalable commodity—sent our sales
through the roof. It was as if we'd uncorked a bottled demand."

Aldy sipped his Malbec, taking in Allen's recount with keen interest. The concept of
packaging Holt's intellectual property in a similar fashion was enticing. As Allen's story
sank in, Aldy contemplated a future where Holt could mirror that instant market trust
by productizing their solutions in a comparable, customer-centric mold.

The Holt team exchanged glances, understanding unfolding in their eyes like dawn
breaking over vineyard rows. Allen had offered them not just insight but an invitation
to play a new game—a game where every dollar spent blossomed into profit under the
nurturing sun of foresight and strategy.

The sun dipped below the horizon, casting a warm glow over the winery's sprawling
vineyards. Glasses clinked, filled with the winery's finest, and conversations flowed as
freely as the wine. Christina leaned forward, elbows on the polished wood of the rustic
table, her gaze fixed on Allen. His casual demeanor belied the weight of his words, and
she was all ears.

"I've got to know," Christina started, her voice a blend of curiosity and urgency.
"How do you manage such a broad customer base simultaneously? The logistics must be
daunting."

Allen's smile held a hint of pride. "Pre-built solutions," he explained, gesturing with an
open hand as if unveiling a hidden secret. "Our first project laid the groundwork. From
there, we constructed a library of reusable components."

Allen's expression turned earnest as he delved deeper into the concept of pre-built
solutions, his hands sculpting the air, emphasizing the framework of his approach. "Imagine a set of building blocks, each designed with precision to address a particular set of
problems within our industry. The first project was all about identifying commonalities
across our customers—repetitive issues, requests, and needs that kept emerging."

His fingers tapped the table, underscoring his point. "We sent our best minds on a
mission to create a highly adaptable platform. It was modular by design, enabling rapid
configuration based on client specifications." Allen leaned back, letting the information

sink in. "We focused on the pain points that every client faced, developed components to solve them, and then we just... plugged and played."

He poured another glass of wine, the rich color reflecting his shining eyes. "Now, we have a comprehensive suite of tools at our disposal. Say a client needs a customer relationship management solution; we pull the corresponding module from our library, tailor it to integrate with their existing systems, and deploy it with minimal adjustments."

Allen paused, allowing for emphasis on the next revelation. "But the true beauty lies in the data models we've built. Because they've been refined through numerous implementations, they're designed to evolve and scale with the client's business. They're robust yet flexible enough to accommodate future growth or changes in the market."

With a sip of wine, Allen capped his explanation. "And there it is—instead of reinventing the wheel with each project, we've cultivated a repository of solutions that are ready to serve. It's about being proactive, not reactive. That's how Optix AI disrupted the market. It wasn't just about speed; it was about delivering a consistently high-quality product that could be deployed globally with minimal friction."

Christina's eyes shone with comprehension, the cogs in her mind visibly turning as she considered the implications for Holt. The strategy Allen outlined could provide them with a crucial competitive edge—a way to capitalize on market demand with precision and agility.

Christina's brow arched, impressed yet probing deeper. "And talent acquisition? Training must be an ordeal with such complexity."

"Not quite," Allen replied, his smile widening. Allen leaned forward, his hands gesturing fluidly as he continued to illuminate the subject. "Our platform's intuitive design simplifies the process. Even those new to the team, the junior developers, can manage deployments with confidence. And at times, the simplicity extends to our clients. With just a brief, focused training session, we can empower a customer's developer to take the reins. After a mere few hours, they're equipped to handle the system independently, making the transition scamless and efficient."

Her mind raced at the simplicity and elegance of it all; such an approach could revolutionize Holt's delivery model. In large organizations, leveraging their existing partners or collaborating with their own preferred partners expedites delivery without compromising quality.

Christina nodded, her thoughts already sprinting ahead to how they could integrate such strategies at Holt. Allen had painted a picture of efficiency and scalability that resonated with her engineering mindset—solutions that could not only solve problems but also anticipate them.

The group fell into a contemplative hush, the kind that fills a room with heavy thoughts and unspoken calculations. Each member swirled their wine, its rich aroma a stark contrast to the dense air of deliberation. Allen broke the silence with the ease of someone who'd mastered his craft.

"We also priced it creatively," he continued, leaning forward with a spark in his eye. "Our cloud-based solution comes with full-service management; we assume responsibility for both the infrastructure and software on behalf of our clients. To enhance the offering, we conduct quarterly cost optimization reviews on their technology expenditures. Moreover, we seamlessly integrate new software features at no extra charge and ensure their hardware remains current with complimentary updates, provided they entrust us with the complete management of the solution.."

Anto's eyes snapped to Allen's face, her posture stiffening. "For free?" she exclaimed, her voice cutting through the tranquility like a shard of glass. "How can you accommodate the cost of all these?"

Allen remained unfazed by her intensity. "We architected our entire infrastructure within the cloud, meticulously automating each component of our operations. This innovation reduces costs to a bare minimum, requiring merely a nominal effort to execute the scripts every quarter."

Allen sensed the curiosity, perhaps a tinge of skepticism, that gripped Anto and the others; the Holt team seemed to linger on the edge of comprehension and disbelief. He continued, warming to the subject:

"Imagine, if you will, a system that's virtually self-maintaining. Our DevOps teams have designed the cloud infrastructure to be self-healing and self-optimizing. Using predictive analytics, our systems anticipate issues before they occur, automatically adjusting resources to meet demand without human intervention."

He paused, allowing the information to sink in, then leaned in slightly, his tone steeped in the passion of one who revels in the intricacies of his work.

"We've employed Infrastructure as Code (IaC), which means every aspect of our hardware setup is defined in code, enabling us to deploy and manage servers and databases through automated scripts. This not only minimizes human error but also allows for rapid scalability."

Allen gestured with his hands, an artist drawing his audience into the vision he sculpted in the air between them.

"Our Continuous Integration and Continuous Deployment (CI/CD) pipelines are setup to roll out updates frequently and consistently, with minimal downtime. Updates to our software stack are thoroughly tested in isolated staging environments, then smoothly transitioned to production with the push of a button in the CI/CD pipeline."

He smiled, knowing the next point would hit home with a finance-savvy individual like Anto.

"And from a cost perspective, this automation translates to substantial savings. Our automated resource scaling can dial up computing power during peak times and dial it back down during lulls, ensuring we only pay for what we use. Additionally, we've negotiated bulk pricing with cloud providers, thanks to our scalable utilization."

Allen's description was a window into a profoundly efficient operation. His eyes shone with the certainty of having answered the unspoken questions in Anto's mind, the numbers and projections now aligning with this innovative business model he advocated. The Holt team sat, enveloped in the realization of how profoundly the landscape of cloud computing, when harnessed with vision, could transform the economics of IT operations.

Anto's mind raced; her financial instincts couldn't reconcile the feasibility of what Allen proposed. The numbers, the projections—they all spun in her head, but no question formed on her lips. She sat back, attempting to stitch together this new tapestry of innovative economics that Allen laid before them.

Aldy leaned forward, the soft glow of the winery's lights casting a contemplative shadow across his face. "Tell me more about your company structure and how it is structured internally."

Allen paused, his gaze drifting to the vineyard's expanse beyond the window, as if he could see the framework of his company etched between the rows of grapes. He turned back to Aldy, his eyes alight with the passion of a man who'd built something from nothing.

"Our culture is completely customer-centric," Allen began, hands unfolding as if revealing a blueprint only he could see. "We do everything based on customer feedback and their preferences. Over time, we wove customer feedback into every department."

Aldy nodded, absorbing each word.

"The outcome," Allen continued, "was that customers desired two types of solutions:

    1. business solutions for leaders and

    2. technology solutions for tech heads."

He described how they split their teams—industry solutions that tailored business strategies for each sector they specialized in and technology solutions centralized under a center of excellence.

Aldy's gaze was intent as he prodded further. "Dive deeper into these 'industry solutions' you mentioned. How do they intersect with the needs of different sectors?"

Allen leaned in, the soft light giving his youthfulness a sage-like quality. "Think of industry solutions as custom-fitted attire for various business personas. Each sector wears its own unique set of challenges," he mused. "For instance, in the realm of finance, we tailor secure transaction platforms that adhere to stringent regulations. In healthcare, it's about seamless patient data systems that prioritize privacy and accessibility."

"And the technology solutions?" Aldy asked, his mind already threading possibilities.

"That's our universal toolkit," Allen said with a wink, gesturing as though plucking ideas from the air. "Centralized in our tech hub, our center of excellence develops and refines cutting-edge tools—AI, cloud infrastructure, cybersecurity. These solutions are tailored not just to support, but to elevate any industry."

The Holt team leaned closer. Audrey, her voice tinged with newfound respect, questioned, "So your teams are woven along these lines as well?"

"Exactly," Allen affirmed. "Our sales and marketing personnel specialize in knowing either the pulse of the industry or the heartbeat of technology, synced perfectly with our dual-line strategy. They speak the client's language, whether it's the technical lingo of IT or the strategic dialect of executive decision-makers."

Around the table, heads nodded in unison, understanding the profound simplicity of Optix AI's approach. It was an alignment of bespoke services with universal tech needs, and it was an approach that had every potential to reshape Holt's trajectory.

As the conversation ambled on, blending with the melodious clinks of wine glasses, Aldy and his team gestured animatedly, their dialogue interweaving tales of industry and technology. The winery's lights flickered off reflections of inspired visions and the glint of transformation, signaling the birth of potential industry solutions and the application of centralized tech excellence, all under the night sky's vast canopy.

A light chuckle escaped him as he shared a secret with the room. "We didn't invent any of this." His smile was one of humble acknowledgment. "We picked it up from customer feedback that we collect after every single conversation with them."

Questions flowed like wine from eager lips as the Holt team delved deeper into Allen's model. The conversation ebbed and flowed around them, the rich aroma of oak barrels mingling with their shared enthusiasm for innovation.

As the evening waned, glasses clinked a final time in appreciation of new knowledge and fine wine. They rose from their seats amidst laughter and a sense of camaraderie, leaving behind the dregs of their drinks and an atmosphere charged with potential. The chapter closed on a group united by curiosity and a thirst for transformation, stepping out into the cool night air filled with the promise of change.

BACK TO DRAWING BOARD

CHARTING A NEW COURSE

The conference room at Holt headquarters buzzed with the hum of fluorescent lights overhead, casting a sterile glow on the sleek table that stretched across the room. Tony strode in, his gait measured and purposeful. The others, scattered around the table, turned to him expectantly.

"What did the board members say?" Tony's voice cut through the hum, sharp and clear.

Aldy looked up from his tablet, where he had been reviewing notes from the conference in Las Vegas. "I just asked for more time," he said with a nonchalant shrug. "There was nothing burning at this time, so they were cool."

Audrey leaned back in her chair, her tailored suit immaculate as always. Her eyes locked on Aldy, searching for what lay beneath his calm exterior. "So what is next?" she prodded.

Aldy set his tablet down and leaned forward, clasping his hands together on the table. "Let's put together a dedicated team to come up with something based on what we learned from Allen."

Christina perked up at this, her eyes lighting with recognition. She interjected before anyone else could speak, "Like a framework?"

Aldy paused for a moment, letting the word resonate in the room. "Exactly," he said finally, "a 'framework'." His gaze swept over his team, igniting a silent understanding that spread through them like wildfire. They knew it was time to translate inspiration into action.

Aldy leaned forward, palms flat against the polished surface of the conference table. The intensity in his gaze held his team captive, a silent cue that he had something pivotal to share.

"We've danced around the idea long enough," he began, his voice steady and compelling. "It's time we give our efforts a backbone—a framework."

Audrey tilted her head, a silent question lingering in her eyes. Tony's pen paused mid-scribble. Christina's fingers stilled on her tablet.

"A framework does more than just guide us," Aldy continued, his voice rising with conviction as he swept a look across the room, ensuring he had the undivided attention of his leadership team. "It's the architecture of our innovation—the very blueprint we'll use to construct our future. It ensures we maintain consistency and direction across all departments, providing the scaffolding upon which our collective ambitions can securely climb."

He paused, allowing the words to settle in the room like dust motes in a sunbeam.

"Envision, if you will, an orchestra," Aldy suggested, his hands moving through the air as if to pluck notes from an invisible score. "A gathering of masters, each a ruler in their craft, ready to create an unparalleled concert."

He walked the edge of the table, much like a conductor threading through a throng of expert musicians.

"Now, remove the framework—the conductor's guiding hand, the written scores—and consider what's left?" His query hung in the ensuing quiet. "Innate skill, undoubtedly. Infinite possibility, indisputably. Yet, in the absence of organization, what ensues is chaos. A missed chance for harmony."

Aldy stopped behind Audrey's chair, resting a hand on its back.

"In this company, we're that orchestra. Our framework is the conductor guiding us, the sheet music we follow." His voice crescendoed with conviction. "It ensures every department, every team member, plays their part in unison."

He moved to the room's edge, gaze sweeping over them.

"With it, we can measure progress at every step, adapt when necessary," Aldy said. "Without it... Well, we risk playing out of tune."

The team absorbed his words, envisioning themselves as part of that grand orchestral vision.

"We didn't see that speech coming," Tony admitted with a chuckle that cut through the tension.

"But he's right," Christina chimed in. "A framework bestows upon us the gift of clarity—it guarantees that our innovations are borne of intention, steering us with clear purpose and direction."

Aldy waited for the momentary murmur of agreement to subside before he continued, eager to elaborate on the framework concept. His voice took on an instructive note, a clear signal of imparted wisdom in the offing.

"Consider this framework as the strategic underpinning of everything we do at Holt," he explained. "Like the sturdy beams of a skyscraper, it supports the weight of our ambitions and the breadth of our innovations. It provides structure to our creative chaos, enabling us to channel our efforts effectively."

The team leaned in, captivated by the unfolding vision.

"This framework will encapsulate our goals, methodologies, and metrics," Aldy detailed. "Starting from our mission statement, it will crystallize into our objectives. Not arbitrary targets, but milestones carved out of our strategic vision. Each department will understand how their individual goals align with the broader horizon we aspire to reach."

Audrey's eyes lit up as the puzzle pieces of Aldy's narrative found their places.

"Our methodology within this framework," Aldy gestured toward Tony, his example of a maestro still playing to his audience. "It will outline how we approach problems, integrate new technologies, and disrupt norms. Our methods will be our playbook, from ideation to execution—innovative but replicable and scalable. This uniformity ensures that regardless of the project's magnitude, our core ethos is unmistakable."

A sense of structure was beginning to emerge from what had been abstract, and Aldy pressed the point home.

"And let's not forget about metrics—our system to gauge the tempo of our progress," he said. "These will be built into the framework as well. Not as rigid signposts but as tools of insight, allowing us to course-correct with agility. They'll measure not just financials, but customer satisfaction, team engagement, and our impact on the market."

The notion of such a comprehensive system stirred a buzz among his team—a blend of excitement and sheer potential.

"Lastly, this framework is iterative. It learns and evolves with us, staying dynamic to accommodate the ever-shifting landscape of technology," Aldy informed them, a surety in his tone depicting a vision that was continually expanding.

Aldy's gaze made a deliberate round of the room once more.

"It's more than a plan. It's a living entity that grows from our shared experiences and our combined intellect," he finalized. "It permits us the foresight to anticipate, react, and lead with deliberation."

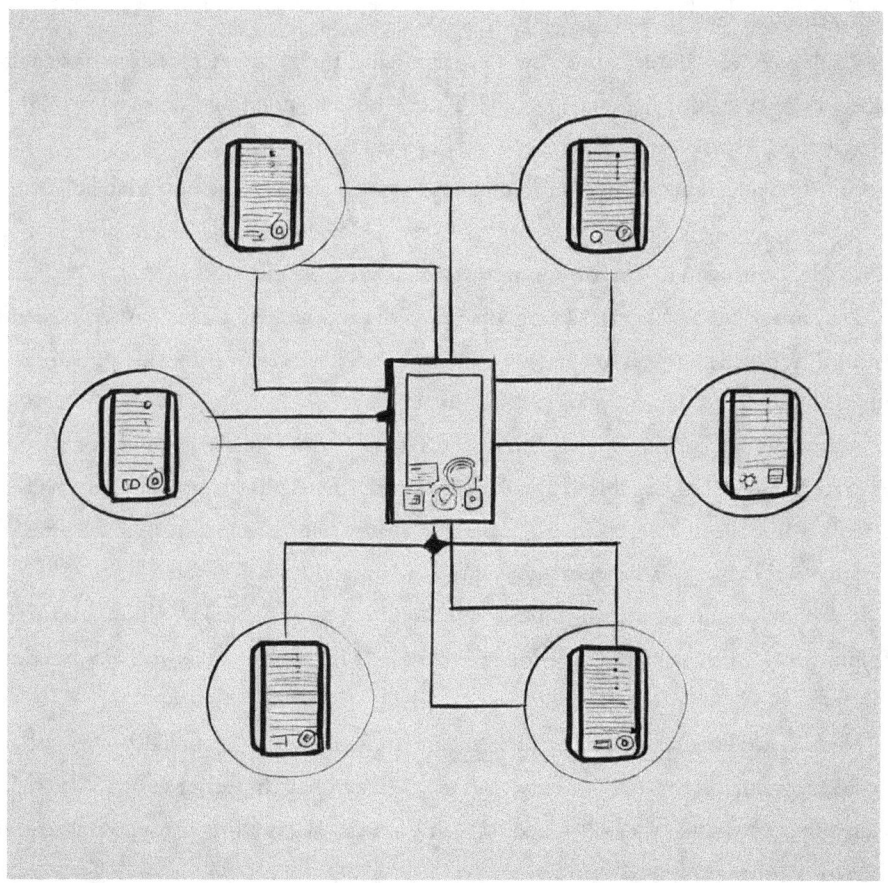

The room fell silent—not with hesitation, but with the weight of responsibility. They understood that the building of this framework wasn't just the erection of a construct but the embodiment of their ethos, a blueprint that would propel them into a future ripe with opportunity and directed by purpose.

Audrey nodded slowly, her earlier hesitation replaced by understanding.

"It's settled then," Aldy concluded with finality. "We build our framework. We create our symphony of success."

They didn't expect Aldy's metaphorical flourish that day but agreed nonetheless; they needed this structured approach to orchestrate their collective talent toward innovation—a symphony waiting to be performed.

Aldy leaned back in his chair, the weight of his words lingering in the air. The team encircling the polished mahogany table mirrored his intensity, each member mentally sifting through their respective responsibilities.

"Audrey, you'll spearhead the customer-facing side. I want you to dive deep into their experience—find out what hits home for them," Aldy said, nodding toward her. Audrey straightened, a spark igniting in her eyes as she jotted down notes.

Christina folded her hands, her mind already racing through the possibilities. "Technology development, engineering, and delivery," Aldy continued, "that's your arena, Christina. I trust you to weave our innovations into reliable solutions."

Tony interlaced his fingers, leaning forward with purpose. "And Tony," Aldy gestured in his direction, "focus on our people and culture. Think about how we can embrace change, both with our customers and within our walls."

Aldy paused, ensuring he had their undivided attention before laying out the next layer of strategy. "We're tackling this with a phased approach. Each phase must deliver a tangible benefit to our clients. Moreover, it's imperative that we weave a customer-centric thread through every stage—gather feedback, refine, and iterate."

The room hummed with unspoken agreement as Aldy concluded. "I don't have to remind you—but I will always prioritize what's in it for the customer in every facet of this framework."

Nods around the table signaled their alignment with Aldy's vision. They knew what was at stake: not just the success of Holt but the satisfaction of those they served. With that shared understanding, they dispersed to their domains of expertise, ready to transform challenges into triumphs.

Aldy locked eyes with Anto, her sharp features softened momentarily by the gravity of the situation. "Can you be part of this as well?" he asked, his voice steady yet imbued with an unspoken urgency. "I want to make sure this is financially beneficial for both Holt and the customer as well. Also, we need some creative ideas for charging the customer differently to solve the low profit margin problem."

Anto's gaze remained unflinching as she processed the request, her mind already churning through figures and possibilities. A slight nod conveyed her commitment; her stance as unwavering as the polished table that separated them.

The room was filled with a collective sense of purpose. Each member stood, shouldering their share of the load, aware of the steep path that lay ahead. They exchanged brief looks that spoke volumes—determination mingled with trepidation, excitement tempered by the weight of responsibility.

As they filed out, their footsteps echoed in the now-empty conference room—a testament to their resolve. The door closed behind them with a quiet click, sealing their pact to innovate and transform, or face obsolescence in an industry that waited for no one.

A NEOTERIC FRAMEWORK

SBF (Solution Building Framework)

Sunlight filtered through the blinds of Aldy's office, casting a striped shadow across his desk. He was engrossed in the latest sales projections when a knock broke his concentration. Looking up, he saw Audrey standing at the threshold, her posture poised and her expression focused.

"Do you have time to chat about the framework?" she asked, her voice cutting through the quiet of the room.

Aldy glanced at the clock on his wall and then back at Audrey. "Sure," he replied with a nod, gesturing for her to enter.

She stepped inside, her heels clicking against the hardwood floor, and took a seat across from him. Audrey laid out a folder filled with charts and notes, pushing it across the desk toward Aldy. The meticulous nature of her work was evident in the organization of each page.

"The team has been hashing out ideas for three weeks," she began, flipping open the folder to reveal a series of flowcharts. "We've come up with three phases for the framework."

Aldy leaned forward, his fingers tapping rhythmically on the polished surface as he absorbed the information before him. "And?" he prompted, encouraging her to continue.

"We're still trying to figure out a name for it," she admitted, brushing a stray lock of hair behind her ear.

Aldy sat back in his chair, stroking his chin thoughtfully. "Let's not get hung up on a name just yet," he said calmly. "Why don't we all meet with the team and go over this? I might have a name for it."

Audrey's eyes lit up with curiosity. She nodded, already reaching for her phone to coordinate with the others. As she exited Aldy's office, there was a shared sense of anticipation between them—an unspoken understanding that this framework could be the linchpin in their company's transformation.

In the conference room, palpable tension hung in the air as the leadership team of Holt waited. Charts and screens adorned the walls, and in the center, a large table hosted an array of laptops and tablets, all poised for the day's critical discussion. Audrey's fingers drummed lightly on the polished surface, betraying her readiness to dive into the presentation.

The door swung open, and Aldy strode in, his hand clutching a thick stack of papers. He surveyed the room with a keen eye, acknowledging each team member with a nod. The soft murmur of conversation died down as all eyes turned to him.

"Are we ready?" Aldy asked, his gaze locking with Audrey's.

Without missing a beat, Audrey clicked the remote in her hand, and the first slide beamed onto the screen. She cleared her throat. "At the core of our framework is our commitment to centering our customers," she began, her voice steady and commanding attention.

"The foundation is built on their feedback; every decision and every step we take is guided by their voices." Her pointer glided over a graph that showed various customer engagement points. "We'll implement customer-centered workshops and whiteboard sessions as our primary delivery mechanisms."

Aldy settled into his chair, his eyes scanning the slide while nodding along to Audrey's words. His presence seemed to amplify the importance of what was being discussed, a silent yet powerful endorsement of Audrey's opening remarks. The room listened intently as she delved deeper into how these strategies would redefine their approach to service delivery and product development.

As Audrey continued to unveil the framework's intricacies, it became clear that this was more than just a new strategy; it was a cultural shift for Holt—a bold step towards becoming a true partner to their clients rather than just another vendor in an overcrowded market.

The conference room's atmosphere buzzed with anticipation of revelation as Audrey unfurled the strategy for the first phase. Her hands glided over the tablet, sending slides onto the screen that held everyone's rapt attention.

"So we broke this into three phases so that we could easily deliver one phase at a time and show value to the customers, which would help them in their transformation," Audrey started, a glint of excitement in her eyes.

Aldy leaned forward, nodding. He sensed the weight of what they were embarking on—a true pivot toward a customer-centric operation.

***

Audrey's voice took on a rhythmic cadence as she laid out the framework.

The presentation pointed to the slide with the title,

Phase 1: Title: 'Insights Lab'—Uncovering Hidden Needs: The Power of Customer Insights,"

Audrey announced.

"Tagline: Discover your customers' world through in-depth research."

"In this phase, we collect the data, do research on the problem, and help them understand what they are really trying to solve."

Each step in the presentation resonated with intent and precision.

The **"Voice of Customer Research"** step, Audrey explained, is a systematic approach to truly understanding the customer's perspective.

"By engaging directly with a diverse range of customers, we can gather authentic feedback and insights that go beyond surface-level knowledge."

She highlighted the following key activities that would be part of the Voice of Customer (VoC) Research:

In-depth Interviews: Conducting one-on-one interviews with decision-makers and influencers to obtain detailed commentary about their business challenges and experiences with related products and services.

Focus Groups: Organizing sessions with customer groups to foster a dynamic discussion environment where participants can build on each other's ideas and viewpoints, revealing new layers of understanding.

Surveys and Questionnaires: Utilizing carefully crafted surveys to gather data from a broader customer base, ensuring statistical significance, and uncovering common trends that may affect the market as a whole.

Customer Observations: Engaging in shadowing or ethnographic studies where teams observe customers in their own settings, using products, or interacting with services to note unspoken behaviors and struggles.

Feedback Channels: Setting up and monitoring various channels such as social media, customer service logs, and online forums to capture real-time customer opinions and concerns.

Net Promoter Score (NPS) and Other Metrics: Leveraging NPS and other customer satisfaction indices to gauge loyalty and overall sentiment towards a brand or product, providing a hard metric alongside qualitative insights.

Customer Journey Analytics: Studying the data on how customers interact with the company's touchpoints to understand friction points and moments of delight in the current user experience.

Audrey, with a clear view of the comprehensive nature of the research, explained how it would involve cross-departmental efforts from marketing, sales, and customer support teams. "This multifaceted approach ensures that we're not just listening, but actively interpreting and analyzing the feedback to extract actionable insights that can drive our Phase 1 solutions."

As she completed the explanation of the VoC Research component, Aldy could envision the immense value in understanding the explicit and implicit customer needs that would shape their offerings. The depth of the research Audrey described was indeed the rigorous beginning they needed for a customer-first strategy.

"**Market Sizing Estimates**," she continued, outlining how they would translate needs into numbers.

Audrey advanced the narrative of their systematic approach by touching on the importance of understanding the size and value of the market segments they intend to serve. "Now, let's discuss the Market Sizing Estimates. It's crucial for us to grasp the potential of each segment to ensure we focus our efforts where the greatest opportunities lie."

She detailed the process:

Total Addressable Market (TAM): Calculating the total revenue opportunity for a product or service if 100% market share is achieved gives us the ceiling for our ambitions.

Serviceable Available Market (SAM): identifying the portion of TAM that Holt can reach with its current products and geographic constraints, offering a more realistic target.

Serviceable Obtainable Market (SOM): Estimating the fraction of SAM that Holt can capture, considering competition and market readiness, thus defining short-term sales goals.

Audrey broke down the methods for gathering data:

Secondary Research: Utilizing existing market studies, industry reports, and competitor analysis to collate data and form baseline estimates.

Primary Research: Conducting surveys and in-depth interviews to fill gaps in existing data, particularly in emerging markets or innovative product categories.

Trend Analysis: Analyzing historical sales data and growth trends within the tech industry to forecast potential market expansion.

"The accuracy of these estimates impacts every aspect of our strategic decision-making," she emphasized, "from product development priorities to sales force allocation."

She also noted the role of market size in resource management.

Resource Alignment: Matching our investment in product development, marketing, and sales efforts with market size to maximize ROI.

Risk Management and Opportunity Cost: Using market size estimates to measure the risk against the potential reward when entering new markets or launching products.

"Understanding market size not only helps us set realistic targets," Audrey concluded, "but it also positions us to be agile, to pivot, and to seize opportunities as they arise in the dynamic tech landscape."

The room absorbed the depth of thought that had gone into this financial aspect of their new strategy, once again impressed with the thoroughness of the upcoming Insight Lab.

"***Competitive Benchmarking***," where they'd juxtapose their clients against rivals to spotlight Holt's unique edge.

Audrey then guided the room's attention to the next significant element. "Let's shift our focus to Competitive Benchmarking," she proposed, unveiling another key part of their ground plan. "We need to understand not just where we stand but also how our clients stack up against their competitors to truly offer them tailor-made solutions."

She outlined the pivotal facets:

Competitor Analysis: Systematically evaluating the offerings and strategies of major competitors in the market to identify Holt's unique value proposition and areas for improvement or differentiation.

Feature Comparison: Detailing a side-by-side assessment of features, benefits, and shortcomings to understand where our clients' products or services excel or fall short compared to the market leaders and other competitors.

Performance Metrics: Reviewing industry reports and case studies to collate comparative performance data, such as market share, growth rate, and customer retention, providing a performance context for our clients' positioning.

Pricing Strategies: Analyzing the pricing models of competitors to identify pricing opportunities or the potential need for Holt's products to reposition based on perceived value.

She walked the team through the methodology:

Data Collection: Compiling information from public databases, financial reports, press releases, and product/service reviews to paint a comprehensive picture of competitors' operations and strategies.

Qualitative Insights: Conducting interviews with industry experts, current and former employees, and customers to gather nuanced perspectives on competitors' market standing.

SWOT Analysis: Employing the Strengths, Weaknesses, Opportunities, and Threats (SWOT) framework to craft a structured analysis of Holt's competitive situation.

Market Position Matrix: Using a market position matrix to visualize where each competitor, including our clients, stands in terms of market share and growth potential.

Audrey addressed the process of putting benchmarking into action:

Actionable Feedback: Translating benchmarking data into actionable feedback for product development, marketing, and sales strategies to enhance Holt's competitive edge.

Continuous Tracking: Setting up systems to keep abreast of competitor moves, ensuring an ongoing awareness of trends and changes in the competitive landscape.

Gap Identification: Identifying performance, feature, or capability gaps that can be opportunities for Holt to innovate or capture additional market share.

"This structured approach to Competitive Benchmarking will arm us with actionable intelligence," Audrey declared, signifying its critical role in the larger strategy. "It informs our product roadmaps, shapes our marketing narratives, and sharpens our sales pitches—ensuring our clients see Holt as their ally in staying abreast, if not one step ahead, of their competition."

With that, she allowed her colleagues to digest the comprehensive battle plan that would enable Holt to spotlight its unique edge in the marketplace.

"**Persona Development**," detailing user archetypes with such vividness that they seemed to walk among them.

Audrey continued with unwavering focus. "Next, we have 'Persona Development.' It's a strategic pivot where we translate customer insights into vivid user archetypes. These personas will guide us in crafting solutions that resonate profoundly with our intended audiences."

She laid out her vision:

Demographic and Psychographic Integration: Drawing from our research to stitch together demographic data like age, occupation, and location with psychographic aspects such as attitudes, interests, and motivations to build multidimensional characters.

Behavioral Patterns: Diving into the data gathered from interviews, observations, and other VoC activities to identify patterns and common behaviors, informing the day-to-day experiences and pain points of our personas.

Empathy Mapping: Using empathy maps to represent the personas in their environments, giving us a glimpse into what they see, hear, think, and feel. This helps develop empathy, a crucial ingredient in customer-centric innovation.

Audrey elaborated on the development process:

Storytelling: Writing narratives that capture a day in the life of each persona, giving weight to their background, challenges, and goals to make them relatable and memorable for the team.

Collaborative Creation: Bringing in cross-functional teams from marketing, sales, and product development to contribute to and validate the personas, ensuring they're accurate and usable across all departments.

Persona Evolution: Committing to an iterative process where personas can evolve based on ongoing customer insights and market changes, keeping them current and relevant.

"In essence," Audrey explained, "our personas are more than mere profiles; they're vibrant, living guides that inform product strategy, marketing messaging, and sales approach. They help us to step into our customers' shoes and view our solutions through their eyes."

As her presentation drew to a close, the room reflected on the detailed process, appreciating the care taken to ensure these personas would not be static caricatures but dynamic and integral to Holt's client-centered transformation.

> "**Journey Mapping**," she narrated, tracing paths through customer experiences that Holt's solutions could elegantly pave.

"Journey Mapping" beckoned her audience to visualize the customer's experience through a meticulously drawn map, showcasing their path interactions with Holt's solutions.

"Journey maps are powerful tools that delineate a customer's full experience with our brand, from the first touchpoint to the ongoing relationship," Audrey elucidated. "They capture the story of the customer's experience."

She described the granularity involved:

High-Definition Touchpoint Mapping: Identifying each stage of the customer's interactions with Holt, whether it's an ad impression, a sale call, or a service review, to create a detailed journey map.

Emotion Overlays: Plotting the emotional highs and lows that customers experience at various stages, these overlays provide depth to the maps, helping us to empathize and respond to customer emotions effectively.

Path Interconnections: Acknowledging that journeys are rarely linear, we'll identify where paths cross or diverge and where customers might loop back due to inquiries or issues.

"Journey mapping provides a coherent narrative that is invaluable for cross-functional team alignment and for honing in on what truly matters to our customers," she added.

In her detailed approach to analyzing these maps, Audrey covered:

Qualitative and Quantitative Synthesis: Balancing the narratives collected through VoC methods with the hard data from analytics to generate a composite view of the customer experience.

Service Blueprinting: Extending journey maps to include back-end processes that impact the customer experience, fostering an understanding of both the visible customer-facing elements as well as the internal actions triggering them.

Continual Validation: Regularly revisiting and updating the journey maps based on fresh data to ensure they remain accurate and reflective of the current customer experience.

"We're crafting routes through the customer's world, identifying boulevards of simplicity and back alleys of frustration. Journey mapping isn't a one-time project," she was keen to emphasize; "it's a continuous practice, evolving as our business and customers evolve."

"With these insights," Audrey concluded, "we can begin to transform these experiences, smoothing the roads and lighting the pathways, so every journey with Holt is an enriching one."

The room listened intently, clearly seeing the merit in such an extensive dive into the customer psyche, with Audrey painting a clear picture of how comprehensive journey mapping would feed into the customer-first transformation they were envisioning.

Finally, **"Use Case Identification,"** distilling their insights into tangible scenarios ripe for transformation.

Finally, Audrey addressed "Use Case Identification," distilling their insights into tangible scenarios ripe for transformation.

She exuded command as she explained, "What we embark on here is the vital process of converting our rich tapestry of data and insights into specific, relatable scenarios—our use cases. These are practical blueprints that define how a customer interacts with our products and services, pinpointing where we can innovate to add tangible value."

"Detailing Scenarios:"

Real-World Context: Drawing from our research, we create detailed scenarios that mimic real-life challenges our customers face, grounding our solutions in practicality.

Problem-Solution Narratives: Each use case narrates a specific customer problem and illustrates how Holt's offering can provide a solution, offering clarity on the benefits in a way that resonates with customer needs.

"Cross-Functional Workshops:"

Ideation Sessions: Engaging diverse teams in brainstorming workshops where we collectively identify and develop use cases that reflect both customer pain points and market opportunities.

Silo-Breaking Collaboration: Encouraging members from different departments to contribute, breaking down silos and fostering a shared vision that incorporates various perspectives for holistic use case development.

"Validation and Refinement:"

Customer Feedback Loop: Presenting the proposed use cases back to customers for validation, ensuring they align with their expectations and address their needs accurately.

Iterative Enhancement: Using feedback to continuously refine our use cases, ensuring they remain relevant and compelling as the market evolves.

"Strategic Alignment:"

Business Goals Integration: Ensuring each use case supports Holt's broader strategic objectives, from growth targets to customer experience improvement goals.

Investment Justification: Using the use cases to guide where and how we invest our resources, ensuring alignment with the most impactful customer needs.

"The culmination of this process," Audrey shared with a sense of satisfaction, "is a suite of use cases that not only speak directly to our customers' needs but also serve as a driving force for Holt's product development, marketing, and sales strategies."

Aldy watched as Audrey masterfully controlled the room with her insights, demonstrating the need for a meticulous exploration of market landscapes—tying potential solutions back to real voices and quantifying every aspect with unwavering discipline. With a succinct summary nod, she handed the floor back to Aldy, her presentation a complete and encouraging blueprint for how Holt's new customer-first strategy would unfold.

Aldy watched her control the room with her insights, feeling pride swell within him. She was driving home the point of a meticulous exploration of market landscapes—tying potential solutions back to real voices and quantifying every aspect with unwavering discipline.

As Audrey concluded her segment on defining success and identifying organizational roadblocks, Aldy couldn't help but interject. "What is the deliverable for the customer? What is the feedback we would ask them?"

There was a brief silence before Tony weighed in, his voice steady and assertive. "The deliverable for the first phase, Aldy, will be an *'Insight Report'*—a comprehensive document that synthesizes all the data and analyses from the Insights Lab," he stated unambiguously. "This report will include a detailed breakdown of the identified needs, the inferred hidden challenges, and our recommendations for the next steps."

Tony paused for a second, ensuring he had everyone's attention. "As for feedback, we'll be asking the customer to validate our findings and share any additional insights that could refine our understanding. We will provide them with a structured feedback form that prompts specific responses on the clarity, relevance, and completeness of our analysis.

Tony concluded, with his hands, to form an arch, as if framing a problem. "Isn't there a saying, 'A problem well stated is half solved'? When they get to see where they are struggling, they will either correct us or agree that it needs to be solved. In our approach, we also highlight the challenges and roadblocks to the organization's readiness to solve them. It would be easy for them to present it to their investors or stakeholders."

Aldy's expression showed he was pleased with the response, the clarity of deliverables, and the feedback aligning with his vision of actionable and customer-focused outputs.

Aldy couldn't contain his excitement. "That's wonderful. Now I can't wait to hear the other phases." His anticipation was palpable; he sensed they were on the cusp of something revolutionary for Holt.

***

The slide transitioned smoothly, reflecting the well-oiled machine that was Audrey's presentation. The title emerged in bold letters:

"Phase 2: Ideation Garage to Co-Create."

Below, the tagline affirmed their mission:
"Innovative solutions that deliver real results for customers."

Abruptly, the focus of the room narrowed as Audrey initiated the next phase of her presentation. "Now that we've harnessed comprehensive insights from Phase 1, we possess exact problem statements that are refined and loaded with potential. It's time we edge forward into the heart of solutioning—the Ideation Garage."

She clicked, and a complex problem statement appeared on the screen, articulating a real-world challenge faced by one of their clients. "Here, we see a crystallized issue, meticulously constructed from our compiled VoC Research and Data Analytics," Audrey gestured towards the statement that summarized the client's predicament clearly and concisely.

"Our value proposition is built upon this foundation," she continued, her fingers tracing an invisible arc from the problem statement on the screen to an unseen point of innovation. "This marks our transition from understanding to action, from data collection to targeted value delivery."

Aldy nodded, his expression one of concentrated interest as he studied the problem statement.

"Let's dwell on **'Framing the Challenge'**,"

Audrey said pointedly, tapping the laser pointer onto the carefully worded problem statement. "Our stakeholder interviews and strategic workshops have revealed underlying systemic issues—those that are often masked by everyday operational distractions."

She advanced to a new slide titled "Unlocking True Value." It featured a flowchart that progressed from the problem statement to a series of targeted questions designed to drill into the essence of the challenge. "We dive deeper beyond the immediate pain points, employing '5 Whys' methodology to dissect and decode the systemic roots of these challenges. This is critical—understanding the framework of the issue before we even begin to ideate solutions."

Audrey allowed for a beat of silence, illustrating the significance of the approach, her gaze sweeping across the room, engaging her colleagues. "Our SWOT Analysis comes into play here, squarely focused on the articulated problem. Its strength? It pulls the context into sharp relief, mapping out not just the immediate issue, but also the surrounding environment that feeds it."

Another slide clicked into place, highlighting priority issues tagged with strategic and feasibility filters. "The selection process is rigorous—filtering the critical from the significant, the impactful from the peripheral. As we dissect and prioritize, we must remain vigilantly aligned with our value proposition, ensuring that the solutions we seek will not only resolve but also enhance and elevate the client experience."

She paused, a visual of ripple effects spreading across the slide, representing the systemic impact of solving for the articulated problems. "This isn't just about fixing; it's about architecting change that propels our client forward, triggering positive waves throughout their organization. With this refined lens, we step into the heart of our Ideation Garage, equipped and ready to co-create not just solutions, but tomorrow's market leaders."

"Drawing from the deep well of insights gathered, we're no longer grappling with hypotheticals," Audrey asserted, "We're engineering precise value propositions that address these refined challenges. Here in Phase 2, our ideation isn't guesswork; it's guided innovation, shaped by verified client realities and a sharp focus on tangible outcomes."

Her eyes then connected with those of each team member, her conviction mirrored in their attentive expressions. "We embark on 'Envisioning the Outcomes' to shape a future that is compelling not only for Holt but for the industry at large. We shall co-author success stories with our clients, narratives that will define strides and foster legacies. Together, we create more than solutions—we mold a future ripe with innovation, primed for our next pivotal leap."

"Next, we 'Envision the Outcomes.'

Imagine a world post-solution; what does it look like? We quantify business metrics and qualify experience improvements. This isn't just about numbers; it's about painting a picture so vivid that our customers can see their future success."

Audrey let the statement linger for a moment to sink in, then continued with a tone of passion.

"We're talking about building a detailed forecast model that shows revenue uplifts, cost savings, and efficiency gains. Setting up this vision involves benchmarking against industry standards and constructing a narrative that vividly tells the story of the customer's journey with the implemented solution."

She gestured towards the next visual that popped onto the screen, showing a vibrant storyboard layout.

"It's about creating that compelling narrative through customer success stories, tying back to the problem statement. We outline specific outcomes, such as 'X percent reduction in operational costs' or 'Y percent increase in customer satisfaction.' But we go deeper—we describe what that success feels like on a day-to-day basis, how it impacts customer relationships, employee engagement, and even the broader industry."

Tony interjected to add depth to the concept. "This visualization phase is critical. It encompasses various simulation techniques and predictive modeling, where we can actually demonstrate potential outcomes based on different strategic decisions, always aligning with the meticulously framed challenges."

Audrey appreciated Tony's interjection and nodded affirmatively.

"We conduct a kind of pre-mortem analysis as well, envisioning risks and obstacles, ensuring we're not just optimistic but realistic and prepared. By identifying potential hurdles beforehand, we can plan our risk mitigation strategies and adapt our solutions preemptively."

She tapped the screen, bringing up a matrix diagram. "See this? We map out a 'success pathway,' detailing the incremental victories and checkpoints along the way. This keeps our strategies agile and focused, letting us measure progress against those vivid outcomes we've painted."

Audrey concluded this segment with conviction in her voice, "Ultimately, by envisioning the outcomes, we're not just selling a product or service; we're co-authoring a future success story for our customers, one that they believe in and are ready to adopt."

Tony leaned forward, interlocking his fingers, the focus of the room centering on him. "When we brainstorm ideas, we're digging for the company's superpower—their unique strength. That's our starting point for leveraging and building upon. Every company has its own set of distinctive capabilities and assets that set it apart from the competition. It's essential to identify and understand these core competencies, as they're the foundation on which we can construct a competitive advantage."

He paused, surveying the room, making sure his point was resonating with everyone.

"These unique strengths could be anything from proprietary technology, a dedicated customer base, robust data analytics, to an agile development team. It's that 'special sauce' that gives them an edge. During our brainstorming sessions, we zero in on these attributes and ask ourselves, 'How can we amplify this? What new opportunities does this open up? How can we align this with customer needs to create something truly exceptional?'"

Tony gestured emphatically, underscoring the importance of this phase.

"It's about taking what's already working and elevating it to the next level—using it as a launchpad for innovation. From there, we envision new applications, new markets, even new business models. This isn't about reinventing the wheel; it's about taking that wheel to places it's never gone before."

He nodded at Audrey, who was following his words closely.

"We delve into ideation with these superpowers in mind, ensuring that we're not diverging from what the company does best, but instead, we're using their strengths to their maximum potential, turning them into robust solutions for the customers."

"Then comes '**Conduct Concept Sprints,**'"

Audrey continued, her eyes sweeping across the team. "We throw everything on the table—every wild idea—before refining and evaluating them for viability. This is the time when creativity must reign supreme, and no suggestion is too outlandish. It's the stage in our process where innovation thrives on spontaneity and quantity, letting the best ideas rise to the top through natural selection."

Audrey's fingers danced in the air, mimicking the sparking of ideas. "These concept sprints are structured yet dynamic brainstorming sessions, time-boxed to ignite urgency and focus. We take the insights gathered from our customers and challenge each other to think divergently, generating a wide array of concepts."

Tony chimed in again. "We can't forget culture—it's crucial. We weave in their mindset, adapt to new technologies and patterns, making sure it feels like their brainchild as much as ours. This iterative process ensures that we're not only creating potential solutions but also embedding them seamlessly within the client's cultural fabric."

Christina added her piece seamlessly, "And when we 'Identify Technologies' during these sprints, we aren't just matching solutions to problems. We're looking ahead, forecasting the technological landscape, and assessing how emerging technologies could provide a competitive edge."

Audrey followed up, nodding in agreement. "These sprints are where the rubber meets the road when it comes to practicality. We rapidly develop prototypes and mockups that bring our ideas to life, allowing us to test and learn quickly. This hands-on approach helps us sort through our ideations, refining them into actionable concepts that we can present back to our customers with confidence."

She emphasized the importance of this step. "In these sprints, customer feedback is our gold standard. We involve them early and often, using their input to steer our development. It ensures that what we create not only meets the challenge but is also aligned with the customer's vision and expectations."

Tony propped his elbows on the table, leaning into the conversation. "The key to these sprints is maintaining momentum and objectivity. Ideas are scrutinized, tested, and either fleshed out or filtered out. It's a fast-paced environment where decisiveness and agility are the name of the game."

Audrey concluded this section of her presentation with a clear sense of direction. "The journey from inspiration to implementation is iterative and collaborative. Our aim? To cocreate high-potential wins that align with customer values and ROI expectations."

The next slide shows with "**Identify Technologies**"

Christina spoke up, a clear thread of excitement in her voice. "And when we 'Identify Technologies,' we're not just matching current needs but anticipating future challenges. Our engagement with cutting-edge tech isn't superficial—we're delving into artificial intelligence, machine learning, IoT, automation, and blockchain to understand how they can not only solve present issues but also pave the way for new avenues of business."

Audrey nodded, her gaze taking in the attentive faces around the room. "Our sprints explore the horizon of tech advancements. We evaluate how emerging technologies can be harnessed to enhance our customers' competitive edge. For example, we look into AI capabilities for predictive analytics that could help a business anticipate market trends and customer behavior."

Christina seamlessly picked up where Audrey left off, her analytical mind sifting through the tapestry of innovation. "We also recognize the power of cloud computing in offering scalable and flexible infrastructure solutions. By 'Identifying Technologies,' we're essentially investigating how these can be custom-built or adapted into our framework to support more responsive and agile business operations."

Audrey resumed, her voice filled with assurance. "In these sessions, we closely work with our in-house tech experts and even partner with tech startups to gain deep insights. While identifying technologies, we ensure that chosen solutions meet stringent criteria for scalability, interoperability, and adherence to the highest security standards."

She emphasized each point with a decisive click, transitioning the slides as she outlined the process. "Our technology identification is also guided by a principle of 'future-proofing' the solutions we offer, ensuring that they not only serve immediate goals but are robust enough to evolve alongside our clients as the market shifts."

Tony interjected with a practical note. "In our concept sprints, we are not only technologists; we are visionaries who align these technologies with the client's strategic roadmap. This means considering regulatory compliance, integration with existing systems, and the ability to leverage data in meaningful ways that drive actionable insights."

Audrey continued, "As we 'Identify Technologies,' we craft detailed roadmaps for implementation, taking into account the need for custom software development or the application of off-the-shelf solutions. We prioritize user experience and the impact on staff productivity, planning for seamless integration and minimal disruption."

She concluded with a high note of innovation and practicality. "This step is pivotal in our process. It transforms theoretical brainstorming into something concrete. It's here where we match provocative thinking with pragmatic execution—taking bold ideas and crystallizing them into leading-edge tech solutions that move businesses forward."

Audrey paused, her gaze piercing each team member. "This is where they recognize Holt as a leader in tech innovation—a pivotal moment.

She stepped closer to the projector, her presence commanding the room. "We're building more than just a portfolio of services; we're fostering a perception that positions Holt at the forefront of the tech revolution. It's about being seen as a visionary entity, one that others aspire to emulate. By closely aligning with our customers' futures, we forge a path that others will want to follow."

A moment of silence settled as the weight of her words sunk in, then she continued.

"When clients speak of Holt, they won't just reference a vendor that provided a service; they'll discuss a partner who envisioned a future with them, who brought disruptive ideas to life and mounted the cutting-edge of progress. We will have built a legacy of transformation and innovation, a testament to our collaborative spirit and forward-thinking mindset."

Audrey's eyes were unwavering, filled with the fervor of her conviction. "Our work here marks a sea change for the industry and for Holt. As we define the standard for business technology solutions, we shift from being participants in this industry to leading it. We're not waiting for the next big tech wave; we're the ones creating it."

She let those last words echo a challenge, not just to her team, but to the industry at large. "Our commitment to innovation, to understanding and exploiting the full potential of emerging technologies, will set us apart. Holt's name will become synonymous with ingenuity and progress. This is how we define our era of leadership in tech innovation—a pivotal moment, indeed."

"Architecting with Agility,"

Tony read aloud from the next slide, his tone conveying the importance of the concept. "We construct solutions with the foresight that change is the only constant. Our designs must be nimble, enabling quick adaptation to market shifts and evolving customer needs."

Audrey nodded in agreement. "This means building our solutions with a modular structure, allowing for seamless updates and enhancements. Modularity ensures that our clients can stay abreast of advancements without overhauling their entire system."

"The agility we engineer into our solutions goes beyond just the technical," Audrey continued. "It's also embedded into our methodological approach. We architect our engagement strategies to be fluid, so we can pivot and respond promptly to client feedback and market changes."

Tony elaborated, emphasizing strategy. "By 'Architecting with Agility,' we optimize for the present but design for the future. Our solutions are not rigid constructs; they're ecosystems that grow and evolve. This is what enables our clients to scale swiftly and efficiently."

Audrey added, her voice tinged with enthusiasm as she projected a diagram displaying a network of adaptable components. "This architectural philosophy also allows us to re-purpose successful solutions across different industries. Each module can be reconfigured to meet diverse challenges, providing a foundational strategy that can be customized as per individual client requirements."

Tony highlighted the practical aspects, his gaze steady. "Within this agile framework, we're looking at things like microservices architecture, which allows us to isolate changes to a particular service without impacting the entire system. It's about creating resilience so that our solutions are not just robust, but also retain their integrity and performance under rapid evolution."

Audrey stepped forward, as the visual transitioned to show an evolving framework. "Our role as architects does not end with implementation. We continue to partner with our clients, maintaining and improving the solutions through ongoing analytics and performance feedback. Agility means being in a constant state of refinement, ensuring continuous alignment with business goals."

Audrey's presentation shifted, as real-world examples of modular architecture at work filled the screen behind her. She pointed to the first case study highlighted on the slide.

"Take, for example, the success story of ABC Logistics. They implemented a modular software architecture that allows for individual components of their supply chain man-agement system to be updated without downtime or system-wide interruptions. This meant that when they needed to implement a new, more efficient routing algorithm, it was simply a matter of plugging in a new module. Their business continued without missing a beat, and they saw a 20% increase in delivery efficiency."

She clicked to the next slide featuring another example.

"Or consider XYZ Bank's customer service platform," Audrey continued, "where using a modular design allowed for the personal banking module to be upgraded with AI chatbots for better customer response times. The rest of the system remained unchanged, which minimized risks and allowed the bank to offer state-of-the-art service without extensive costs."

The audience took note as the next example came into view.

"And there's DEF Healthcare," Audrey explained, "which adopted a modular infrastructure for its patient management system. This modular setup enabled quick integration of telehealth services during the recent health crises, providing continuity of care despite the surge in remote consultations. This not only improved patient satisfaction but also expanded their service capabilities."

Tony supplemented Audrey's points. "All these examples showcase how companies capitalized on modular architecture to stay ahead of the technological curve and adapt quickly to new opportunities. These aren't isolated incidents; they're indicative of a broader trend that prioritizes flexibility and responsiveness."

He gestured toward the projection. "Moreover, these case studies reflect how modularity is not confined to software alone. It spans across products like smartphones, with standardized components that can be easily upgraded or replaced, to the construction industry, where pre-fabricated, modular units allow for faster build times and easier maintenance."

Audrey nodded, reinforcing the message. "These are the types of agile solutions we aim to architect. Solutions that are resilient to change, that empower our clients to evolve their operations at their own pace, and to be at the forefront of innovation in their respective industries."

"So when we talk about 'Architecting with Agility,' it's about more than just the end-product. It's a mindset, a strategic approach that imprints adaptability into the DNA of our solutions, fostering long-term innovation and sustained success for our clients."

The slide advanced to "**Validate with Customers**," a step underscoring the imperative of collaboration in the innovation process.

"To ensure that our solutions genuinely resonate with the needs and expectations of our clients, we engage in a rigorous validation process," Audrey began, her voice echoing the critical nature of this phase. "This means establishing direct lines of communication with a cohort of target users, bringing the voice of the customer into the very heart of our development cycle."

Tony added, leaning back in his chair with an air of strategy, "To do this effectively, we establish an advisory board or working group from the client's side. This panel comprises a diverse range of stakeholders, including end-users, IT staff, And customer service representatives, to refine and enhance our solutions together."

Audrey transitioned to the specific methods utilized to gather customer feedback. "Through design workshops, user testing sessions, and beta releases, we gather valuable insights straight from the source. It's about engaging with the customer throughout the creative process, iterating based on their feedback, and ultimately crafting solutions that are not just accepted but embraced by the end-user."

"The results from these validation exercises are taken seriously," Audrey continued, her focus unwavering. "They help us identify potential friction points, refine user interfaces, and even influence the strategic direction of the solution. We chart these findings meticulously, often leading to enhanced feature sets or pivot strategies that align with overarching business objectives."

Tony nodded. "And let's not overlook the importance of facilitating a smooth transition for clients embracing these new technologies. Ease of adoption is pivotal for success, so we invest time in creating comprehensive onboarding materials, training seminars, and interactive learning workshops. This proactive educational approach greatly enhances adoption rates and customer satisfaction."

Aldy listened intently before jumping in with supportive enthusiasm. "Exactly! This phase solidifies our commitment to customer-centric design. Our role extends beyond innovation; we are guides, leading customers comfortably through this new chapter of technological evolution." His affirmation resonated with shared purpose—a team united under a banner of customer partnership and proactive adaptability.

"To do this," Tony added, leaning back in his chair with an air of strategy, "we establish an advisory board or working group from the client's side to refine and enhance our solutions together through design workshops and ideation sessions."

Audrey proceeded with **sizing investments**—

breaking down pricing models to accommodate different budgets while ensuring operational costs were transparent. "Effective investment strategies aren't one-size-fits-all. Each client has distinct financial thresholds and ROI expectations. Our job is to scale and tailor our solutions according to this economic landscape," she articulated, gesturing toward a new slide picturing a tiered investment model.

"On this axis, we map the client's investment against potential returns. It's crucial to frame this within the context of their current spending and long-term strategic goals," Audrey continued. She clicked through to a graph that clearly showed ROI projections over time. "Here's where we make the business case for each innovation strategy by projecting its economic impact, from cost savings to potential revenue generation."

Tony joined in, pointing to a line item on the chart. "These investment models also consider phased roll-outs. Starting with a pilot project allows clients to see the value in a tangible form before committing to a full-scale implementation."

Audrey nodded. "Exactly, Tony. And when we discuss the total cost of ownership, it's not just the initial outlay we're examining. We include ongoing costs like maintenance, training, and future upgrade paths to ensure there are no surprises down the line. This transparency builds trust and long-term partnerships."

"The journey from inspiration to implementation is iterative and collaborative," Audrey reiterated. "Our aim? To co-create high-potential wins that align with customer values and ROI expectations."

Tony emphasized the dynamic nature of their investment approach. "And let's not overlook the mix of capital expenditure versus operational expenditure models. Some clients prefer one over the other, and we are ready with solutions that accommodate both."

Aldy, interjecting with enthusiasm, underlined the importance of financial clarity. "Exactly! Our role is to demystify the investment required to embrace these innovations. We show them the full journey upfront—from initial costs to ongoing benefits—so they can make informed, confident decisions." His words carried the weight of experience and the commitment to transparency that was a hallmark of the team's approach.

"The journey from inspiration to implementation is iterative and collaborative," Audrey concluded. "Our aim? To cocreate high-potential wins that align with customer values and ROI expectations."

Tony nodded. "And let's not overlook easing them into these new technologies through learning workshops—it can make all the difference in adoption rates."

Aldy listened intently before jumping in with supportive enthusiasm. "Exactly! Our role is to guide customers comfortably through this new chapter of change." His affirmation resonated with a shared purpose—a team united under a banner of innovation and customer partnership.

Anto leaned back in her chair, absorbing the pricing models Audrey articulated with her usual composed analysis. As the presentations progressed, Anto's sharp gaze remained fixed on each PowerPoint slide, scrutinizing the financial frameworks underlying each option. Her reserved demeanor revealed little of her thoughts.

However, as Audrey concluded the outcome-based pricing segment and advanced to transition slides, Anto suddenly sat up, her eyes flashing intense curiosity.

"Let's rewind a bit," Anto interjected, an uncharacteristic impatience creeping into her tone. "I want to clarify how the outcome-based model accounts for the total cost of ownership."

Audrey paused, glancing up from her laptop, briefly surprised by the normally reticent Anto's spontaneous query. She nodded for Anto to continue.

"Now, it's not just the technology investment required, correct?" Anto prodded further, peering over her glasses. "There are additional costs: integration, training, and revisions. How do we quantify the value to ensure we don't underestimate expenses?"

Tony added thoughtfully, "Don't forget change management costs as well. Adoption inhibitors from processes to people."

Anto concurred. "We must capture all tangible and intangible costs to safeguard a positive ROI."

Audrey smiled, appreciating Anto's diligence in ensuring pricing models tied directly to Holt's solution capabilities and scoped implementation costs.

Audrey sighed softly and advanced to the pricing slide, which she saved in the appendix, focusing on cost structures. "You guys are spot-on. We want to show them an innovative cost structure—outcome-based pricing."

Eyes around the room fixed on Audrey with keen interest.

"Here are the pricing structures we would present to the customer based on their use case." She proceeded through each model with precision.

As she detailed 'Subscription-Based Pricing,' 'Value-Based Pricing,' 'Tiered Pricing,' and finally 'Outcome-Based Pricing,' Audrey articulated each use case with clarity.

Subscription-Based Pricing: This model charges customers a recurring fee—typically monthly or annually—to access a service or product. It's predictable for both Holt and their customers, encouraging long-term relationships.

For services requiring continuous use or support, such as cloud-based software offerings or ongoing IT support and maintenance services. Customers who prefer predictable budgeting and consistent service levels would find this appealing.

"Take our cloud storage solutions, for instance," Audrey explains. "Clients will have ongoing access to storage resources and support for a fixed monthly or annual fee, ensuring budget predictability and continuous service without the need to constantly renegotiate terms."

Value-Based Pricing: Prices are set primarily according to the perceived or estimated value of a product or service to the customer, rather than on the cost of the product or historical prices.

Ideal for unique or highly differentiated offerings where Holt's solution can significantly improve a customer's revenue or efficiency and where the value can be quantifiably demonstrated.

"Consider our AI analytics platform," Audrey continues. "Its price would reflect the substantial cost savings and revenue growth potential it can unlock for our clients, not merely the cost of development or delivery."

Tiered Pricing: Different price points are set for different levels of product or service offerings. Customers can choose a pricing tier that best meets their needs, often in terms of features, capabilities, or usage limits.

It works well for software products or services where customers might need more or fewer features or varying levels of service or support.

"Our cybersecurity service can be tiered," Audrey suggests. "Basic, Advanced, and Premium levels could offer differing degrees of protection, monitoring, and response services, allowing customers to select the level that suits their security needs and budget."

Outcome-Based Pricing: This innovative model links the pricing of services to the outcomes they achieve for the customer, such as performance improvements or cost savings. It aligns Holt's incentives with customer success.

Suitable for solutions that directly impact a customer's key performance indicators and where those outcomes can be accurately measured and attributed to Holt's offering.

"For our bespoke software development," Audrey could propose, "pricing could be based on the increase in customer engagement or operational efficiency that our solution provides. If our software doesn't hit the agreed-upon benchmarks, the client pays less, tying our compensation directly to their success."

"As we fine-tune our framework, each of these pricing strategies will be matched with particular client scenarios. Our framework is designed to be as flexible and client-focused as our solutions, ensuring that our pricing structures enhance the value proposition and align with the outcomes our clients actually care about."

"The choice of pricing structure depends on factors such as the nature of the services, customer expectations, the perceived value of solutions, and business goals," she explained.

"As we incorporate feedback and analyze data," Audrey concluded, "advanced statistical models will standardize pricing metrics and estimate integration enhancements accurately." Her confident tone echoed her extensive experience in successful sales strategies.

Audrey, aware of the primed curiosity her colleagues held onto after her forward-looking statement, chose this moment to delve deeper into the future possibilities of the statistical model she had introduced.

"With each deployment of our solutions at customer sites, Holt gathers an invaluable dataset," she resumed her explanation, gesturing subtly towards the screen displaying graphs and numbers morphing into predictive curves and models. "This data—from performance metrics to user engagement—is the fertile ground from which our advanced statistical model will grow."

She clicked to a new slide titled "Data-Driven Pricing Model." It showcased a timeline of steps, beginning with the initial client contact and moving through the deployment phases.

"Imagine this," Audrey painted the picture with her words as much as with the visuals projected behind her: "each time we innovate and co-create with a client, we feed that experience back into our model. The more data we accumulate, the more robust and reflective of real-world situations our model becomes. It's a cycle of improvement that accelerates with each iteration."

The slide transitioned to show an infographic: a self-perpetuating loop where "Data Collection" led to "Analysis," then to "Model Refinement," and finally "Deployment & Feedback," which circled back to "Data Collection."

"As we continue to refine our solutions, the data they produce will inform our statistical models. These models aren't static; they are dynamic and evolving. We'll use machine learning to adjust the parameters, enhancing our predictive capabilities and price standardization methods. The more we deploy, the smarter our system will get—anticipating customer needs, forecasting market trends, and setting accurate, competitive prices."

She emphasized how essential it was for Holt to maintain a seamless integration of analysis and feedback, ensuring each customer's unique complexities and the contextual variances they operated within were accounted for.

"We'll build a repository of insights—think of it as a living library of customer experiences," Audrey continued. "This will allow our model to become increasingly precise
over time, offering predictive pricing that isn't just guessing but is underpinned by solid,
historical evidence. And, most importantly, it will be driven by the specifics of each
customer's use case."

With her predilection for hard facts, Audrey was painting a future where Holt's service
offerings could be as tailored and precise as the suits she wore—a future where their
predictive model would become an indispensable part of the sales process, a navigational
tool for navigating the nuanced seas of customer needs and solution delivery.

She nodded firmly, affirming the strategic foresight that would place Holt and its
clients in a position of advantage. "In time, as we fine-tune the feedback loops and enhance
the granularity of our data, we aim to present a pricing model that is not only advanced
and accurate but also transparent and autonomous, allowing our customers to engage
in a self-service experience that is informed by data-driven insights tailored specifically
to them. This, colleagues, is how Holt will set the standard for innovation in pricing
architecture."

Anto sprang from her seat with rare excitement. "Wow! That would be awesome!"

Aldy turned his gaze toward Christina. "Can we build something like this?"

Christina responded promptly and without hesitation. "It's technically possible; we
just need data to build it."

With that confirmation hanging in the air like a promise of progress, Audrey advanced
to reveal another slide, her audience fully engaged in what was unfolding before them.

***

Audrey clicked the remote, and the conference room screen flickered to the next slide.
The header, bold and assertive, declared,

"Phase 3: Solutions Launchpad for Win-Win Launch."

Beneath it, a tagline beckoned:

"Put the customer at the heart of your business."

"This phase," Audrey began, "is where we make it all happen. We've identified the problems, we've shaped the solutions, and now we're on the brink of rolling them out." She swept her gaze across the room. "But let's not kid ourselves—it's not just about pushing code or plugging in hardware. We're deploying business transformers here, so we need to gauge the impact on our end customers meticulously."

Aldy leaned forward. "The users of our clients' products, you mean?"

"Exactly," Audrey confirmed with a nod.

She motioned to the bullet points that materialized on screen.

"First up—'**Clearly Define Value Metrics**.'

We'll need to lay out tangible outcomes that sync with our stakeholders' KPIs and describe qualitative impacts that resonate with them."

Audrey clicked to the next slide, where a structured diagram appeared, dividing the 'Clearly Define Value Metrics' into actionable components.

"We need a systematic approach to define our Value Metrics," she explained. "Here's how we plan on doing it."

She pointed to the first part of the diagram: **Establish Objective Benchmarks** "We'll start by establishing objective benchmarks for each solution. This involves identifying industry standards and creating baseline metrics that help us measure improvements over current client states."

Audrey clicked again, and a bullet point appeared beneath the first: **Set Quantifiable Goals** "Each solution will have clearly set quantifiable goals tied to specific client outcomes. Think along the lines of increased efficiency rates, decreased downtime, or cost savings potentials—numbers that speak volumes."

With another click, another sub-point appeared: **Articulate Value Propositions** "Beyond the quantifiable, we articulate the qualitative value propositions. For example, ease of integration, user-friendliness, or scalability. These are the benefits that capture the client's imagination and showcase our deep understanding of their pain points."

Audrey gestured to a new section on the diagram: **Monitor and Tune Performance Indicators** "Continuous measurement is vital. We'll monitor performance indicators and tune our solutions post-deployment. This allows us to show clients the real, ongoing value our solutions provide, reinforcing their decision to invest in us."

One more click and the final point under Value Metrics shone on the screen: **Tailor Reports for Stakeholders** "Tailor reports to the stakeholders' vernacular and priorities. From an on-the-ground tech manager needing thorough operational reports to the C-suite requiring strategic exec summaries. Tailored reporting ensures our solutions' value is recognized at all organizational levels."

She shifted her weight, emphasizing the need for this granularity. "We're laying the groundwork for a powerful narrative; it's these metrics that will back up our stories of success with hard data, allowing us to build long-standing, consultative relationships with our clients."

Audrey looked confidently around the table at her engaged colleagues. "This, in a nutshell, elevates us from a vendor to a valued partner in our clients' eyes. It's the essence of our Solutions Launchpad."

Aldy nodded, clearly impressed with the depth and thoughtfulness of the plan unpacked before them.

Audrey, engaging with the audience, advanced the slide. "Moving on," she said, her fingers poised over the clicker.

Map Buyer Personas to Positioning "This is about getting into the heads and hearts of each buyer persona. Understanding not only who they are but also how they think and what drives their decisions enables us to align our solutions' positioning perfectly with their expectations."

The screen displayed a detailed breakdown of the process she was describing.

"We start with in-depth persona outlines," she continued, pointing to the first bullet point. **Develop In-Depth Persona Outlines** "To create these profiles, we dive into demographics, job functions, priorities, pain points, preferred channels of communication, and decision-making processes. This isn't about surface-level assumptions; it's data-driven empathy."

The next bullet point focused on messaging. **Craft Targeted Messaging** "Once we understand our personas, we tailor our messages. Each buyer persona receives a narrative that resonates with their specific needs and preferred outcomes, translating features of our product into benefits that speak their language."

Another click revealed the next step. **Align Positioning with Buyer Journey** "How we engage with potential clients changes depending on where they are in the buyer's journey. We introduce, educate, or persuade, tailoring our content and communications accordingly to nurture them through the sales funnel."

Audrey gestured towards a graphic that showed this alignment strategy. **Customize Solution Portfolios** "To further refine positioning, we'll customize solution portfolios for each persona. This means bundling our products and services in a way that makes the most sense for their respective businesses and pain points."

The final bullet point under this section was: **Leverage Influencers and Testimonials** "Every buyer trusts different sources. Identifying and leveraging industry thought leaders, influencers, and existing satisfied clients for testimonials can provide the social proof that different personas need to feel confident in our solutions."

Audrey concluded, "We'll use these insights to position our offerings in a way that is almost irresistible because it feels like it's made just for them. This isn't a one-size-fits-all strategy; it's bespoke solution positioning."

Nods from around the table acknowledged the sophistication of the strategy, and Audrey sensed that they grasped the importance of this personalized approach in their collective plan for the Solutions Launchpad.

She highlighted a third point.

"'**Develop Scalable Pricing Plans**.' This isn't just about competitive pricing; it's about growth. As customers scale, so should their investment in our solutions."

Based on our plan we would pick the right pricing plan for the solution and deliver that.

Develop Scalable Pricing Plans

"We also have the cornerstone of our commercial strategy to discuss: Develop Scalable Pricing Plans. This isn't just about competitive pricing; it's about aligning our services with the growth of our customers."

She clicked, bringing up a new list of detailed bullet points:

Assess Cost Structures "Firstly, we must assess our cost structures to ensure we deliver value while maintaining profitability. This analysis includes fixed and variable costs, ensuring scalability without eroding our margins."

Value-Based Pricing Models "As we discussed earlier, We are going to adopt value-based pricing models which ensure that our customers see the clear ROI from investing in us. This approach will involve setting prices based on the perceived or estimated value to the customer rather than just on our cost to deliver."

Dynamic Tiered Offerings "Implementing dynamic tiered offerings that allow customers to start with a base product and add features or services as their business needs expand. This not only provides a clear path of growth for our customers but also for our revenue."

Flexible Contracts "Next, we will develop flexible contracts that adapt to customer usage and scale. As our clients grow and their usage increases, the contracts can scale accordingly, giving them peace of mind that their costs are aligned with their business success."

Performance-based Incentives "Performance-based incentives are on the docket as well. This pricing plan rewards customers for reaching certain milestones with us, like increased usage or efficiency gains, through discounts or additional services."

Transparent Pricing "Transparency is key in our scalable plans. Customers will always know what they're paying for and why. Transparency builds trust, and that trust paves the way for growth—both theirs and ours."

Aldy plugged in, this is where our new tool would be useful. Christina, Smiled.

Cyclical Review Process "Lastly, a cyclical review process will be in place, where we routinely evaluate our pricing strategy against market trends, customer feedback, and our financial targets to ensure our pricing remains competitive and fair."

Audrey looked around the room as the screen behind her showcased the comprehensive approach to pricing. "This is how we ensure that our pricing strategy is not just about the numbers. It's about fostering a growth journey with our clients, where their expansion fuels our innovation, creating a symbiotic relationship that drives the industry forward."

The team around the table listened, absorbing the intricacies of the multifaceted pricing strategy she laid out. They recognized that this wasn't just a monetization scheme; it was a fundamental piece of the partnership they wanted to build with their clients.

Audrey advanced to the next slide with a sense of pride in her voice:

Arm Trusted Advisors

"Our partners and resellers are extensions of us—they need to know these solutions inside and out. And we've got to make it easy for them—sales tools, licensing know-how—the works."

She paused to allow the new title to sink in, then continued with the detailed bullet points that began to populate the screen:

Comprehensive Training Programs "We start by rolling out comprehensive training programs tailored specifically for our trusted advisors. They'll receive in-depth knowledge on features, benefits, workflows, and the nuances of our solutions."

Access to Sales Enablement Tools "Our partners need to be equipped with state-of-the-art sales tools that help them communicate our value proposition effectively.

This could include interactive demos, detailed product sheets, case studies, and tailored presentations."

Licensing and Configurator Knowledge "They also need a solid grasp of our licensing structures and configurator tools to provide immediate, accurate responses to clients' queries about pricing and customizations."

Regular Updates on Product Evolution "As our solutions evolve, our advisors must remain in the loop. We'll set up a system for regular updates and feedback loops, so our network is always informed about the latest enhancements and offerings."

Dedicated Support Channels "For any questions or challenges they face, there will be dedicated support channels. Our resellers and partners should feel fully supported with priority access to our technical and sales teams."

Rewards and Incentives Programs "Motivation is key. We'll implement a rewards and incentives program that acknowledges the successes of our advisors, deepening their commitment to our solutions and incentivizing exceptional performance."

Marketing Collaboration "Working together on co-marketing initiatives will allow us to leverage their networks and ours for broader outreach and stronger market penetration."

Real-time Analytics and Feedback Tools "Real-time analytics and feedback tools will give them immediate insights into customer behavior and solution performance, enabling them to make smarter, data-driven sales decisions."

Audrey's eyes moved across the room, looking to her colleagues. "These actions won't just ensure that our advisors have the knowledge they need to succeed; they'll make them experts in translating customer challenges into transformational impacts with our solutions."

With confidence and clarity, she outlined an ecosystem that not only empowered their trusted advisors with the tools and knowledge they needed but also fostered a collaborative and mutually beneficial relationship.

As Aldy finished outlining the key areas for enabling their trusted advisors, he pivoted back towards Audrey with an appreciative smile.

"Superb that you already highlighted the immense force multiplication potential from prepared partners, Audrey," he noted, gesturing at the slide. "I should have realized you would snare this vital element."

Audrey smiled back, touched by Aldy's praise. "Of course - our advisors become invaluable extensions of Holt, reaching markets and customers we couldn't alone. Their success fuels our success."

"Exactly," Aldy concurred. "And by comprehensively arming partners to aptly convey our value, we elevate results together."

He swept his gaze across the room. "Make no mistake - achieving our ambitious vision requires commitment to empowering our allies beyond treating them as tertiary considerations."

Aldy's voice swelled with growing excitement. "Because when our partners grasp the immensity of the problems we solve, and the outcomes we deliver, they evolve into evangelists eager to usher in transformation!"

Appreciative sounds resonated amongst the group. Tony added, "And their networks merging with ours creates that crucial tipping point for exponential expansion."

Aldy gestured in endorsement towards Tony. "Yes, an unstoppable groundswell! But it starts with dedicating resources to amplify our advisors' success, as Audrey wisely included."

He lifted his glass towards her in recognition. Audrey accepted it with a knowing smile, as the team aligned on this critical force multiplier undergirding their ambitious ascent.

As the room settled into a focused silence, anticipating the next segment, Audrey looked around and clicked the remote. The following slide projected an attention-grabbing header:

Engineer Low-Friction POE or MVP

She began, "To really gain traction with our solutions, we need to craft an entry that's as smooth as silk for our customers. Here's our plan to engineer a low-friction Proof of Execution (POE) or Minimum Viable Product (MVP) that makes trying our solutions effortless."

Audrey highlighted each step with a corresponding bullet point on the screen:

Free or Low-Cost POC "We'll offer free or low-cost POC to let potential clients experience the benefits firsthand without a heavy investment. It's the test drive before the purchase – showcasing the solid performance of our solutions."

Money-Back Guarantees "To build trust and lower the risk barrier even further, we'll stand behind our solutions with money-back guarantees. If our solutions don't meet their needs or expectations, they won't lose out for trying."

Streamlined Onboarding "Once a client decides to trial our MVP, we'll have a streamlined onboarding process in place. This means minimal paperwork, fast-track implementation, and dedicated support to get them up and running quickly."

Output-Based Pilots "Aiming to highlight the tangible outcomes of our solutions, we'll structure pilots focused on achieving defined, measurable results within a set period."

Customizable MVP Options "Our MVPs won't be a one-size-fits-all. We'll offer customizable options tailored to the unique needs of each customer, ensuring relevance and immediate value."

Feedback Loops and Rapid Iteration "Early and ongoing feedback is gold, and we'll set up systems to capture this critical input. It enables rapid iteration, ensuring our MVP aligns closely with customer needs and delivers on its promises."

User Experience (UX) Focused Design "UX is paramount. We'll design our POE and MVP with a laser focus on user experience, ensuring it's intuitive, engaging, and error-tolerant, reducing friction and encouraging continued use."

Outcome-Based Marketing Material "Our marketing will reflect the low-friction entry point. Educational materials will outline clear expectations, success stories will demonstrate potential, and clear calls to action will guide prospects towards trying our solutions."

Audrey stood back, the proposals reflecting in her eyes as much as they did on the screen behind her.

"We want the experience of trying our solutions to be so compelling, so hassle-free, that moving forward with us is the obvious next step. Our job is to make adoption feel like the natural progression – to confirm that investing in Holt solutions is the best business decision they can make."

She waited a beat before concluding on this point, ensuring the gravity of this approach settled within the room.

Audrey shifted gracefully to the final slide in her presentation, signaling another critical element of the Solutions Launchpad. With each click, her confidence seemed to infuse the room with anticipation. The header materialized on the screen:

Staff Client Success Teams

"We understand that post-sale engagement is as crucial as the initial sale itself," she began. "That's where our Client Success Teams come into play. They're not just support staff; they're customer advocates. And here's how we make sure they're prepped to deliver impeccable service from day one."

Audrey highlighted the key components of the strategy with each bullet point:

Intensive Solution Training "Our success teams receive intensive training on our solutions, not only from a technical standpoint but also understanding the business impacts and customer goals."

Proactive Relationship Management "They actively manage the customer relationship, anticipating needs, and obstacles, and offering solutions before they become problems."

Onboarding and Training Excellence "Every new customer will experience a seamless onboarding process and receive comprehensive training modules tailored to various roles within their organization."

Ongoing Support and Education "Continuing education is just as important as initial training. Our Client Success Teams will offer webinars, Q&A sessions, and custom training as our solutions and the customer's understanding evolves."

Metrics-Driven Accountability "Each team member will have clear metrics tied to customer satisfaction, retention, and growth, ensuring accountability and continuous enhancement in how they serve our clients."

Cross-Functional Collaboration "Our Client Success Teams will work in close collaboration with product development and sales to provide feedback directly from customers, helping to guide our solutions' evolution."

Customer Advocacy Programs "Building community is vital. Our teams will manage customer advocacy programs, celebrating successes, and transforming our customers into champions of our brand."

Customizable Support Packages "To ensure we meet varied needs, we'll create tiered support packages. Customers can choose the level of support that fits their needs best, ensuring they feel valued no matter their size or spend."

Empowered Decision-Making "Our Client Success Teams will have the authority to make certain decisions on-the-spot, reducing customer friction and enhancing the overall experience."

Personalized Communication Channels "We'll utilize the customer's preferred communication channels—whether that's email, chat, phone, or video conferencing—to ensure they can reach us on their terms."

Audrey's presentation underscored a well-thought-out approach to customer service that signaled to the team the kind of superior experience Holt was aiming to provide.

"So there you have it," Audrey said, wrapping up, "a top-tier client success initiative that ensures customers not only achieve their goals but also become loyal advocates for Holt. It's how we close the loop on the Solutions Launchpad and ensure our solutions continue to deliver value long after the deal is done."

As she finished, the assembled team exchanged looks of mutual respect and agreement, each of them visualizing how these components would play out in reality, securing success for their customers and Holt alike.

She stepped back and surveyed her colleagues.

"We're not just selling a product; we're guiding customers through every stage—from awareness to purchase to expansion. Our aim? To spark a cycle of continuous value and use that doesn't end with the sale."

Audrey paused before concluding.

"So that's the gist of it—the framework we've crafted." She flashed a confident smile. "We're still batting around names for this beauty, though."

***

As the final slide from Audrey's insightful presentation faded from the screen, a collective sense of achievement settled over the room. Phase three of the solution-building framework had been meticulously detailed, painting a comprehensive vision of the new customer-centered framework that promised to lift Holt to bold new heights. The team leaned back in their chairs, faces lit with the glow of the projector, digesting the wealth of information that had just been laid before them.

Aldy allowed the silence to linger for a moment, acknowledging the gravity of what they were on the cusp of. They had the architecture of revolution at their fingertips, but they needed the keystone—what to call this transformative strategy. He knew that to move forward, they needed something to rally behind—a name that would encapsulate the essence of their collective endeavor.

"So," Aldy broke the silence, shifting the focus from reflection to action, "we have our strategy, we have our method. Now, what do we call our brainchild?"

The room stirred, as if awoken from a spell cast by Audrey's final words. This was a new challenge, a different kind of creative process that required the distillation of complex concepts into a single, powerful term.

Suggestions started to bounce around the room. Some proposed technical terms, coined to convey the analytical prowess of the approach, while others leaned towards more abstract concepts, crafted to evoke emotional resonance.

The conversation ebbed and flowed, from pragmatic to poetic, from specific to grandiose. And yet, nothing quite stuck. Each suggestion, while valuable, failed to capture the full spectrum of innovation and customer partnership that they were striving for.

It was then that silence once again claimed the conference room, as if the team collectively ran through their mental thesaurus and found them wanting. The weight of expectation loomed large, now compounded by the fatigue of the long hours they'd spent in strategic warfare.

In this stillness, with the unspoken understanding that they had yet to find their name,. Suddenly, Aldy's voice shattered the stillness. "Neoteric!" he exclaimed, and as abruptly as he had spoken, he fell silent. The room remained frozen for a moment longer, his team turning to him with puzzled expressions.

He leaned forward, hands flat on the table, his eyes gleaming with the fervor of revelation. "That's the name," he declared.

His team exchanged uncertain glances. Neoteric? The term was unfamiliar, yet it hung in the room like a charged particle.

Aldy unfolded his hands and sat back, a confident smile spreading across his face. "Neoteric," he began, enunciating each syllable as if to let them taste its novelty. "It comes from Greek roots—neo for new, and teros implying youth or freshness."

He paused, letting the etymology sink in before continuing. "According to Merriam-Webster, it signifies something modern, new, innovative. Isn't that precisely what we're aiming for with our framework? To infuse Holt with fresh energy and groundbreaking ideas?"

His colleagues nodded slowly as they absorbed the meaning. Aldy pressed on with growing enthusiasm.

"Imagine it—**Neoteric**: a beacon signaling our shift from the old guard to pioneers of customer-driven solutions. It's catchy too; once you hear it, it sticks."

He leaned in closer, as if sharing a secret strategy. "But this is more than just semantics—it's about ethos. Neoteric will be our map through uncharted territories of customer challenges. It'll guide our brainstorming sessions, our design thinking sprints, even our validation processes—all while keeping our clients' needs at heart."

Aldy swept his gaze across his team. "It's about shaping an innovation factory—a consistent pipeline for crafting solutions that resonate with our customers instead of scurrying after market trends."

His voice gained momentum like a drumbeat, propelling them towards an inevitable victory march. "Neoteric will make us agile collaborators, not just vendors transacting goods and services."

He rose from his chair, palms pressed down on the glossy surface as if steadying himself against the surge of his own vision.

"I see us releasing bold solutions under Neoteric's flag—solutions that change the game for us and our customers alike."

His team looked on, their initial puzzlement morphing into nods of understanding and flickers of excitement.

"Think it over," Aldy concluded with an air of finality yet inviting collaboration. "Let's reconvene soon to discuss how we'll launch Neoteric into Holt's ecosystem."

As they filed out of the conference room one by one, Aldy remained behind for a moment longer. He gazed out through the floor-to-ceiling windows at the horizon beyond—a tangible frontier waiting for them under Neoteric's guiding star.

ZERO TO ONE

POWER OF FOCUS

A week had rolled by like fog dissipating under the morning sun. The Holt conference room hummed with a latent energy as Aldy took his place at the head of the table. Audrey walked in, her brows knitted, lips pursed in a clear display of concern.

"I'm stuck," she admitted, breaking the anticipatory silence as she took her seat. "We have the framework but... I'm not sure what to do with it."

Aldy leaned forward, hands clasped on the polished wood before him. "Let's test it out," he said with an immediacy that left no room for doubt. "Let's see if this works in the real world."

Audrey's eyes widened; her panic was palpable. "Are you sure? What if we fail? What if customers get confused and we end up tarnishing our brand image? We need to think this through before taking it to market. Should we hire a consulting firm to validate and give us a green light?"

Aldy paused, considering her words. The silence stretched, but within it, he found clarity. "No," he finally said, his voice resolute. "Let's test it with one customer—how about Doll Inc.? Mark is a good friend; he showed interest in our solution-based approach at the conference."

The tension that had clung to the room's edges began to dissipate. Tony chimed in with a nod of approval. "That's a good idea; it might work. And if we fail, Mark isn't going to hold it against us."

Heads around the table bobbed in agreement.

Christina then leaned in, her voice steady and certain. "Let's start with 'Conversation Intelligence to enhance customer service.'" She recalled how her team had successfully implemented this solution for another client before—a triumph that still resonated within Holt's corridors.

"That could be particularly interesting for Mark since he leads customer experience at Doll Inc." Her statement hung in the air, heavy with possibility.

The team exchanged glances of newfound confidence as they rallied behind Christina' suggestion, ready to embrace this challenge head-on. They were embarking on uncharted waters, yet the current of their collective resolve promised to carry them forward into a future where their framework would not just exist but thrive in the real world.

The aroma of charred meat mingled with the smoky sweetness of bourbon as Aldy ushered Mark into his favorite restaurant, a place where the ribeye reigned supreme and the atmosphere hummed with a low-key sophistication. Audrey and Christina trailed behind, their expressions a blend of anticipation and curiosity.

The group settled into plush leather chairs, the clink of fine cutlery punctuating their arrival. Aldy watched Mark's face light up as he scanned the menu, eyes pausing on the ribeye, a hint of a smile creeping across his face.

"Mark, this place does justice to a good steak," Aldy said, nodding toward the menu. "Their ribeye's a masterpiece."

"And their bourbon selection isn't too shabby either," Mark replied, his voice rich with approval as he lifted his glass in a silent toast to the evening ahead.

As dishes arrived and conversations ebbed and flowed, Aldy leaned forward, capturing Mark's attention. "We've been cooking up something at Holt, not quite ribeye, but I think it's just as exciting," he began, laying out the framework of "Neoteric," their freshly minted customer-centric operation strategy.

Aldy, with a twinkle of excitement in his eyes, straightened and began his pitch with the charisma of a seasoned leader. "Mark, Neoteric—our new strategy—is all about empowering customers through direct engagement and customized solutions. We're moving past generic support, diving deep into data analytics to predict and fulfill customer needs before they even knock on our door."

Audrey, with a tendency to remain anchored to the tried and tested, detailed the proposition with a hint of skepticism, yet she couldn't hide her intrigue about the potential benefits. "Now, I'll admit, I'm a traditionalist at heart. But even I see the edge in what we've got here with Neoteric. It's our platform where we gather customer data, analyze it, and get ahead of the curve. This isn't just another 'innovation.' It has the legs to redefine how we understand—and satisfy—our customers."

Christina, whose pensive demeanor underscored her analytical mind, contributed her technical insight. "What we've engineered behind the scenes is a suite of tools integrating AI and machine learning. These aren't just buzzwords, Mark. They are the scalpel we'll use to carve out solutions that fit our clients like a glove. By infusing our products with actionable intelligence from the Neoteric, we can provide not just what's requested, but what's required, at a pace and precision the industry hasn't seen before."

Aldy picked up on the momentum, drawing Mark's attention to the big picture. "Imagine implementing Neoteric at Doll, Inc. Your customers will feel like they're not just heard, but understood. And that's a game-changer in customer service. You won't be just solving problems; you'll be preventing them, fostering loyalty that pays dividends."

Mark, skeptically nodding along, was curious yet cautious. "It sounds like you've got it all figured out. What you're proposing is a significant shift from our current operations. How do you suggest we integrate this without disrupting our ongoing services?"

Aldy, prepared for this, replied confidently. "That's the beauty of Neoteric. It's designed to be phased in. We'll start small—a pilot project tailored specifically for one segment of Doll, Inc. This allows us to show proof of concept and tweak as we go. Risk is managed, and your ongoing services remain unscathed."

Audrey added, "And from a sales standpoint, this approach doesn't just retain clients; it draws new ones in. They see innovation and commitment to their success—it's a powerful message."

Christina closed the discussion with a definitive nod. "Plus, it's a collaborative effort. My team will work closely with yours to ensure seamless integration and continuity. We're in this together."

With the three Holt leaders outlining the potential of Neoteric, the framework's holistic focus on customer relationships and service was clear. Aldy's vision, Audrey's sales expertise, and Christina's technical precision presented a compelling argument for Mark to consider a partnership with Doll, Inc.

Mark listened intently, his relaxed demeanor untouched by the weight of the discussion. As he savored another bite of steak followed by a contemplative sip of bourbon, he glanced around at Aldy and his team—faces alight with passion for their project.

"I love that you guys are stepping up," Mark said finally, his words slow but sure. "I want you guys to succeed and help us transform as well." He leaned back in his chair, letting the ambiance cushion his words.

The table shared a collective chuckle as Mark added with a wry grin, "I'll do everything I can unless you guys don't get me fired."

Aldy raised his glass in response, his eyes crinkling with mirth. "We wouldn't dream of it," he assured. "Here's to not getting fired and to forging new paths together."

Glasses clinked in agreement, sealing the pact amidst laughter and the warm glow of possibility that stretched out before them like an endless horizon.

***

The Doll headquarters buzzed with activity, a hive of professionals orbiting a central conference room where Audrey had laid out her offerings of peace and goodwill in the form of coffee and donuts. She straightened the stack of neatly printed agendas beside the refreshment table and checked the digital clock on the wall. The room settled as her team took their seats, exchanging brief, expectant glances.

The projector hummed to life, casting a glow on the screen as Audrey and Christina's meticulously crafted presentation materialized. It was a dance of charts and bullet points choreographed to illuminate Holt's new customer-centric operation framework, **"Neoteric."**

Tony slipped into the room unnoticed, finding refuge in a shadowed corner just as Audrey commenced her walkthrough. Her voice carried through the space with precision, detailing the intricacies of their framework without plunging too deep into the weeds.

After twenty minutes, a silence hung briefly before Audrey gestured toward the Doll team. "Let's dive into each phase together," she said, inviting collaboration.

Mark was the first to speak up. His voice held an edge of urgency as he outlined a surge in customer complaints—a cacophony of dissatisfaction that had crescendoed over recent years.

The tension in Mark's voice was palpable as he began detailing the crux of Doll Inc.'s predicament. He described a troubling and relentless increase in customer complaints that had turned into a crescendo of dissatisfaction, much like an unwanted symphony reaching its peak.

Mark's polished facade betrayed his concern; the steady rise in grievances over the years had not only stained the customer service department's stellar record but also hinted at deeper, systemic issues within the products or service protocols themselves.

"For too long, we've been hearing the discord," Mark admitted, a discernible urgency threading his words. "Our clients' frustrations have been mounting, spanning from product issues to displeasing customer service encounters. This is more than an anomaly; it's a pattern, and it's threatening the trust we've built."

As Mark elucidated the breadth of the dissatisfaction—product malfunctions, inefficient service, and tangled customer relations—it became clear that his department was overwhelmed, struggling to pinpoint a clear starting line for addressing the myriad issues. It wasn't just the direct complaints that were concerning; it was the underlying factors that remained elusive, resisting the solutions his team had applied thus far.

Audrey, poised and attentive, acknowledged his concern with a thoughtful nod as she considered the multifaceted nature of the problem—a problem that the "Neoteric" framework sought to untangle systemically, from the very first touchpoint to the after-sales support. She was poised to delve into the Neoteric phased approach, ready to offer a bespoke response to the very challenges Mark had laid bare.

Audrey absorbed his concerns with a nod, her mind already weaving through the data she had gathered on Doll Inc. With finesse, she peeled back layers to reveal underlying goals and pain points specific to Mark's department.

The projector's soft hum faded into the background as Audrey turned towards Mark's team, her eyes reflecting the depth of her preparation. "Before we dive into the details of 'Neoteric,' I want to share the research and insights my team has gathered about Doll Inc.," she began, her voice steady and confident.

Mark and his team leaned in as Audrey recounted an exhaustive analysis of Doll Inc.'s market position. "We've combed through years of your customer service records, identifying not just the frequency of complaints but the nature of each issue," Audrey mapped out the methodical approach, "This quantitative data was then cross-referenced with the emotional feedback gathered from focus groups and surveys. It wasn't just about figuring out what was going wrong, but why it was impactful to your customers on a personal level."

Her presentation shifted to graphs and pie charts, representing competitive benchmarking outcomes that contrasted Doll's offerings with those of their rivals across various metrics, such as customer retention and product innovation. "Understanding your position in the market is key. We looked at where your products outshine the competition and—more critically—where they don't," she disclosed the results, inviting nods of understanding around the room.

The intensity in the conference room notched higher as she discussed the sentiment analysis conducted on customer interactions. "The tone, the words used, the narrative—they all tell a story. We decoded that language to capture the actual sentiment of your customers, their disappointments, and expectations," Audrey continued, highlighting the novel approach her team took.

"You'll find on your tables the latest market intelligence we added this morning: trends that may impact your landscape, emerging technologies, even potential disruptors." Audrey gestured towards the neatly placed documents in front of each member of Mark's team, indicating the diligent updates that accounted for the ever-changing market dynamics.

As Mark's team scanned through the documents, appreciative murmurs filled the space. The real-time data snippets laid out a stark, current image of Doll's customer relations, feeding directly into the narrative Audrey was crafting.

Audrey met Mark's gaze, now flickering with a newfound respect. "With each layer of analytics, our aim was to construct an understanding of Doll Inc.'s challenges that was as granular as it was comprehensive. What we present today with 'Neoteric' is a framework not just informed by data but sculpted by it, tailored to address Doll Inc.'s specific hurdles and aspirations."

The room lapsed into a contemplative hush, the weight of Audrey's research evident in the air. Mark's team, once sceptical, now appeared poised to embrace the new insights and direction that Audrey was proposing. They were no longer just spectators of a presentation; they were active participants in a conversation that could redefine the future trajectory of Doll Inc.

As they spoke, Tony observed from his corner, his analytical gaze flickering between Audrey and Mark. He noted how Audrey guided Mark with gentle yet deliberate questions, coaxing out the information necessary to tailor their approach.

Tony watched as Audrey leaned in slightly, her tone both curious and purposeful. "Mark, can you detail your current customer journey as you understand it, including the pain points where satisfaction dips?"

Mark, rubbing his chin thoughtfully, responded, "The onboarding process is smooth, but there's a gap when transitioning to our support team. We're seeing drop-offs in satisfaction—users feeling left on their own to navigate complex features."

Audrey jotted down notes before replying, "That's valuable insight. How does your team gather feedback post-resolution?"

"We've relied on satisfaction surveys," Mark admitted, "but response rates are low, and I suspect they don't capture the full spectrum of client emotions."

Nodding, Audrey glanced over her notes. "Understood. Let's explore how to enrich that feedback loop and ensure it reflects the entirety of the customer experience. "

Tony held his contemplative gaze on them, recognizing this exchange as a critical link in fortifying their strategy.

When they paused for coffee, murmurs filled the room—a mix of concern and curiosity—and Tony leaned back against his chair, considering the unfolding dynamics with interest.

The clink of coffee cups punctuated the quiet of the break room as Audrey leaned against a high table, her gaze settling on Mark. "You think they'll bite at Doll? Big old companies, they don't pivot on a dime."

Mark sipped his coffee, his eyes narrowing thoughtfully. "Tough, yeah, but not impossible. The higher-ups are starved for fresh ideas. There's this... hunger for change."

Audrey's brow arched. "Even with the behemoth of tradition they're lugging around?"

A chuckle escaped Mark as he nodded. "Exactly because of that behemoth. We're at a point where if we don't shift, we'll be left behind. The board knows it. They're itching for a strategy that's both innovative and viable."

"So," Audrey pressed, tilting her head to one side, "if we bring them a solid business case..."

"They'll listen," Mark affirmed with a confidence that seemed to infuse the air.

"And who exactly are we talking to?" Audrey queried, her pen poised over her notepad.

Mark began outlining the key players at Doll Inc., each name accompanied by a brisk sketch of their corporate persona. "Well, there's Helena—CFO. Numbers are her language; she'll want forecasts and figures that sing profitability. Then you've got Raj—Head of Tech Operations. He's all about scalability and security."

Audrey jotted notes feverishly as Mark continued. "Samantha, our CMO, she'll want to know how this aligns with the brand and impacts customer perception."

"And Greg?" Audrey asked, knowing he was the CEO.

"Visionary," Mark replied succinctly. "He'll need to see how 'Neoteric' not only solves problems but also drives us into new territory."

"Got it." Audrey circled Greg's name on her pad. "So our pitch... it's gotta be a symphony, hitting all the right notes for this diverse audience."

"Exactly," Mark agreed.

Audrey leaned back, absorbing this information like a sponge soaking up spilled tea. "And how do decisions usually flow at Doll? Any idea on team dependencies when it comes to rolling out these solutions?"

Mark traced an invisible chart in the air with his finger. "Think waterfall and spider web combined. Ideas start at the top but spread out through committees and departments—each with their own say."

"So it's vital we understand those connections," Audrey mused aloud.

Mark nodded in agreement. "The smoother we can make those intersections between teams, the better our chances."

With each detail Mark provided about Doll Inc.'s decision-makers and their operational dynamics, Audrey saw clearer paths through the corporate maze—a maze she was determined to navigate with finesse.

Christina stood at the head of the room, her eyes scanning the collection of faces before her. The quiet hum of anticipation lingered in the air as she prepared to dive into the complexities of their new endeavor. Her voice, clear and authoritative, sliced through the silence.

"So, let's talk tech," she began, tapping her stylus against the tablet cradled in her arm. "I want to know everyone's thoughts on what we've seen today. How do these innovations align with our vision?"

One by one, Christina fired off questions, each a precision-guided missile aimed at uncovering weaknesses and opportunities within their strategy. Her inquiry probed into preferences for platform integration, security protocols, and potential scalability issues.

Christina raised her hand, signaling the first of her many queries. "How do we envision a new solution integrating with our clients' existing platforms without causing major disruptions?"

As a few attendees began to scribble down some thoughts, Christina continued, her tone forensic and unyielding. "We've seen a lot of potential in advanced encryption technologies today. What are the implications for our security protocols if we incorporate these into our solution?"

Without missing a beat, she moved onto the next point of contention. "Considering the diagnostic AI we've been impressed by, what scalability challenges might we face if we implement such a system company-wide?"

She paused briefly to let the gravity of her questions sink in, then resumed, "We've witnessed the rise of blockchain-based solutions. How feasible is it for us to adapt our infrastructure to fully leverage blockchain for transaction security?"

Christina's gaze was intent as she addressed another critical point. "I want to talk about our data storage strategy in light of what we learned today. How do we ensure that as we scale, we maintain performance and compliance across the board?"

She tapped her tablet a few more times, reviewing her list. "We've also talked about edge computing as a means to enhance our IoT offerings. What would be the first steps to integrate this with our current suite of services for seamless user experience?"

By now, the room was alight with the buzz of conversation as each leader reflected on Christina's questions, considering the implications of each technological opportunity and challenge presented.

Tony leaned back in his chair, his gaze flicking from Christina to each respondent. He folded his hands together, a contemplative expression etched onto his face. The weight of their task settled heavily on his shoulders as he watched Christina orchestrate the discussion.

'This is difficult,' he mused silently. The myriad opinions and interests in the room spun a complex web of challenges. His eyes settled on Mark, who navigated the conversation with a diplomat's grace, yet Tony could see the strain behind his polished veneer.

As ideas ricocheted around the room, Mark steered them toward consensus with an adept hand. Yet even he couldn't mask the undercurrent of tension that came with managing such a diverse group of leaders.

Hours slipped by as they cataloged technology preferences and debated potential applications. Audrey scribbled notes feverishly, her pen dancing across paper as she captured every detail of the conversation.

Finally, as dusk painted shadows across the conference room walls, they reached a natural pause. Audrey looked up from her notes and addressed the room.

"Okay folks," she said with an authoritative nod. "I'll compile all this and send it out tomorrow morning for feedback."

She then turned to Mark and his team leads who had remained engaged throughout the meeting. "Let's get Phase 2 on the calendar," she suggested with a mix of resolve and fatigue in her voice. "We need to define our solutions based on what we've gathered here."

Mark nodded in agreement, his eyes meeting Audrey's with a silent understanding of the task ahead. They exchanged quick details before adjourning for the day.

The group dispersed slowly, leaving behind an empty conference room charged with silent potential—a tableau poised for innovation and change.

***

The morning light slanted across the conference room, casting elongated shadows of chairs and tables across the polished floor. The team, convened once more in this familiar space, settled into their seats with a sense of purpose. Christina stood at the head of the table, tablet in hand, her eyes reflecting the resolve that had brought them all together.

She launched into her presentation, outlining the solution her team had meticulously crafted. "We've developed a platform that combines advanced AI diagnostics with blockchain technology for enhanced security," Christina began, tapping her tablet to bring up a series of diagrams. "It's designed to integrate seamlessly with existing systems, providing a layer of intelligence that optimizes operations and strengthens data integrity."

Christina explained how the platform leveraged modular architecture, allowing clients to select and implement components as needed. She emphasized its scalability, from small businesses to large enterprises, and its capacity for real-time analytics that could predict maintenance issues before they occurred.

"This isn't just about staying current; it's about leading the charge," Christina stated firmly. "We're talking about a system that not only enhances operational efficiency but also revolutionizes customer interaction through its predictive capabilities."

Questions began to fly from around the table like arrows aimed to test the strength of Christina's proposal.

"How will we ensure compatibility with legacy systems?" one colleague probed.

"Can you guarantee the AI won't produce false positives?" another challenged.

"What about data privacy concerns with blockchain transparency?" came another question.

Each query was met with precision and patience. Christina parried with examples and case studies, detailing how similar challenges had been overcome in other industries.

Yet despite her thoroughness, skepticism hung in the air, palpable as the tension in a taut string. Colleagues drilled down on potential weak points, questioning the platform's cost-effectiveness and market readiness.

Tony observed from his corner of the room as Christina navigated the onslaught. His expression remained unreadable until he sensed a crescendo in the room's energy—a critical mass that threatened to derail their collective progress.

Raising his hand slightly to catch their attention, Tony suggested a pause. "How about we take a coffee break?" His voice cut through the cacophony like a knife through butter. Reluctantly, heads nodded in agreement.

In the break room, Tony steered Audrey and Christina aside. "We need to align our strategy," he said softly but with an underlying steeliness that commanded attention.

The trio huddled together as Tony shared his thoughts on reframing their approach to ensure it resonated with everyone's concerns. By the time they returned to the conference room, there was an air of collaboration rather than conflict.

Tony didn't resume his position at the front; instead, he pulled up a chair beside the lead architect and addressed his colleagues laterally. They all leaned forward slightly, anticipating his words.

"Let's go back to the drawing board," Tony proposed calmly but assertively. "Let's redefine our goals and outcomes for Holt." He looked around at each face in turn. "We need a shared vision—one that we all believe can redefine our place in this industry."

Silence fell upon them—a silence not of defeat but of contemplation—as they considered Tony's invitation to rebuild their strategy from the ground up. It was an acknowledgment that while they had traveled far on this journey of innovation, there was still work to be done before they could reach their destination.

A hush fell over the room as Aldy turned to the lead engineer, his eyes gleaming with the spark of an idea. "Could you sketch that out for us?" he asked, motioning to the expansive whiteboard that dominated one wall of the conference room.

The engineer nodded, a small smile playing on his lips as he stood. The room's attention followed him as he approached the board, uncapping a marker with a decisive snap. Words and diagrams began to flow from his hand, each stroke methodical and purposeful. The engineer's movements wove a narrative of possibilities and potentials, the inked points a map of where they could go.

From across the table, the Doll Inc. architect watched, captivated by the unfolding blueprint. She leaned forward, her eyes narrowing in concentration as she interjected with probing questions.

"Have we considered how edge computing could streamline our data processes here?" she asked, pointing to a section of the whiteboard.

Christina's gaze followed the architect's finger. "We've been exploring that," she replied, her voice steady. "Edge computing could indeed minimize latency for real-time analytics."

The architect's nod was thoughtful as she scribbled notes onto her own pad of paper. Suggestions flowed from her lips with an eagerness that was contagious. Christina fielded each query with expertise, her answers painting a clearer picture of how these technologies could mesh seamlessly into their strategy.

Mark sat back in his chair, arms folded across his chest, eyes wide in amazement at the symphony of ideas blossoming before him. The Doll technical team was aligning on a vision that echoed Christina's initial proposal so closely it was uncanny.

Meanwhile, Tony played the role of inquisitor flawlessly. His questions cut to the core of each topic like a scalpel, carving out clarity from complexity.

"How will we ensure data integrity across platforms?" Tony asked, leaning forward to catch every nuance of the response.

"And what about scalability? As we grow, how does this solution adapt?" he continued, each question spurring deeper thought and collaboration among the teams.

Amidst this whirlwind of technical discourse sat Audrey, pen flying over paper as she distilled high-level concepts into digestible insights. She was the bridge between worlds—translating complex jargon into summaries that would resonate with those not present.

The workshop drew to a close, with both teams radiating satisfaction. They had arrived at an innovative solution—one that bore Doll Inc.'s fingerprints yet was deeply rooted in Holt's original vision.

As they stepped through the doorway into the fading light of day, Audrey couldn't contain her excitement any longer. "This is awesome!" she exclaimed. "They came up with the solution themselves."

Christina's smile was one of triumph mixed with relief as she replied smoothly, "Now they can't complain about it; it's their idea based on ours." Her words carried weight—the weight of ownership and buy-in from their new partners at Doll Inc., marking a milestone in their collaborative journey.

***

Audrey burst into Aldy's office, her breath short, a wild energy in her eyes. Papers clutched in her hand fluttered like the wings of a startled bird.

"You won't believe the turns we took in that workshop," she gushed, pacing the length of the room. Her hands gestured vividly as she recounted each moment. "We've twisted and turned every concept, challenged every norm."

Aldy watched her from his desk, an amused glint in his eye. He leaned back in his chair, letting her enthusiasm wash over him.

"And the proposal," Audrey continued, tapping the stack of papers against her thigh. "It's ready, Aldy. It's solid, and it's bold."

She halted in front of his desk, eyes locked on his. "We're taking this to leadership. Your presence there—it'd mean everything."

Aldy stood up slowly, a smile curving his lips. "I wouldn't miss it for the world."

In the polished confines of the Doll Inc. office, the atmosphere hummed with the gravity of potential change. The boardroom, a bastion of decision-making, welcomed Greg Doll, CEO, alongside his trusted CFO and an assembly of VPs. They convened with an air of expectation as Mark took his place among them, his suit a testament to the occasion's significance.

Aldy entered the room flanked by Audrey and Tony, their presence marked by an aura of preparation and purpose. The presentation equipment hummed to life as Aldy approached the head of the table where Greg sat, poised with an attentive gaze.

"Good morning," Aldy began, his voice steady and imbued with a respect that echoed off the boardroom walls. "I'm Aldy, CEO of Holt. Today we're here not just to share a vision but to fortify a partnership—one that Mark has been instrumental in nurturing."

He allowed his eyes to linger on each face around the table before continuing. "Mark's insights have been invaluable to our understanding of Doll Inc.'s commitment to excellence. Together, we're poised to elevate that commitment in ways that will redefine customer service and satisfaction."

Aldy's speech was more than just words; it was a testament—a pledge of trust woven from shared goals and mutual respect. His tone resonated with an earnestness that drew nods from around the table.

With the foundation laid, Aldy gestured toward Audrey, who rose with confidence, her preparedness palpable. She clicked through to her first slide—a sleek design that mirrored Holt's cutting-edge approach.

"Our vision," Audrey started, her voice clear and composed, "is rooted in understanding and exceeding your customer's expectations." The screen displayed an elegant roadmap—fluid yet precise.

"We propose rolling out our strategy in phases," she explained. "Each phase is a bite-sized entry point designed for measurable impact." The plan unfurled on screen: phases named Discovery, Integration, Optimization—each marked by milestones.

"Considering end users," Audrey continued, "is paramount. We've outlined a comprehensive training program followed by continuous support." Her finger traced over charts showing a user-friendly transition from legacy systems to their innovative solutions.

Audrey shifted seamlessly into costs—a topic often fraught with tension—yet her delivery remained engaging. "Our cost structure," she assured them with a hint of pride in her tone, "is transparent and crafted for value." She outlined competitive pricing models juxtaposed against projected ROI figures that seemed almost too enticing to question.

"Neoteric isn't just a framework—it's a catalyst for evolution," she concluded with conviction. Her gaze swept across the room like a maestro commanding attention for the final note of a symphony.

As she clicked off the projector, leaving the Doll executive team in contemplative silence, it was clear: Audrey's proposal wasn't just compelling; it was crafted to turn skeptics into champions.

In the Doll Inc. boardroom, a palpable sense of excitement hung in the air as the Holt executives concluded their presentation. The meticulous details of the "Neoteric" framework had not only been heard but truly understood by the Doll leadership. Eyes gleamed with recognition of potential, and an energy of eagerness to act pervaded the space.

"This is an amazing framework; we should copy it from you guys," exclaimed the Doll VP of Sales, unable to hide his admiration. His voice carried the weight of a compliment that resonated with his peers.

Greg Doll, seated at the head of the table, remained silent for a moment, his demeanor as composed as ever. His nod was subtle but affirmative, an unspoken endorsement that spoke volumes.

The CIO turned towards Mark, his gaze direct and piercing. "Have you talked to your team and the technology director to get approval for this?"

Mark straightened in his chair, the gravity of the question not lost on him. "Not yet. We need your blessing first to start sharing with anyone at Doll Inc."

"Let me know when you schedule the meeting; I will join to support," said the CIO, offering a level of backing that underscored the significance of what was unfolding.

With final handshakes exchanged and mutual congratulations filling the room, everyone began to depart. There was an air of disbelief that lingered—a marveling at how swiftly and decisively a large company like Doll had embraced such a transformative initiative.

Once approval had been granted, Phase 3 leaped into action, with both Holt and Doll teams rolling up their sleeves. They plunged into implementation with fervor, knowing that success hinged on their commitment and collaboration.

Every other week, like clockwork, status reports circulated between teams. Progress was charted with meticulous precision as each milestone was approached with dedication and every hurdle navigated with shared resolve. The fusion of Holt's innovation with Doll's legacy was more than a partnership; it was a testament to what could be achieved when vision met opportunity head-on.

FROM SELLING TO SOLVING

REIMAGINING THE COMPANY

A ldy sat in his office, the hum of the building's central air providing a steady back-drop to his thoughts. His gaze lingered on the cityscape outside, tracing the sharp lines of Silicon Valley's skyline. The phone rang, shattering the calm.

"Hey Aldy!" Mark's voice boomed from the speaker. "I just wanted to thank you for the initiative. It's going great; our leadership is happy, and we're seeing some early success with our customers as well."

A small smile tugged at Aldy's lips. This was the news he'd been anticipating.

"Your team has done a great job of working so closely with us and providing all the support we need," Mark continued, warmth in his tone. "You guys have shown up as true strategic partners."

Aldy leaned back in his chair, relief and pride mingling within him. "Mark, that's fantastic to hear. We aimed to exceed your expectations, not just meet them."

Mark chuckled. "Well, you've certainly done that. And hey," he added, a note of intrigue coloring his words, "our CIO, whom you met, wants to talk to you about another initiative they're thinking about. It sounds like a big one, so get prepared."

The smile on Aldy's face broadened into a grin as he jotted down a reminder on his notepad. "Big is what we do best," he replied with confidence.

They exchanged a few more pleasantries before ending the call. Aldy stood up and walked to the window, his reflection superimposed on the bustling city below. He felt a surge of anticipation for what lay ahead—another challenge, another opportunity to lead Holt into uncharted territory.

He turned from the window and strode toward the conference room where his team awaited; it was time to share the good news and prepare for the next big leap forward.

Aldy convened the meeting with a ring of optimism that resonated through the sleek conference room at Holt headquarters. The usual pre-meeting murmurs gave way to attentive silence as he began, his voice carrying the weight of a milestone achieved.

"It's been a long time since I got a call from the customer like this," Aldy started, locking eyes with his team. His smile was infectious, spreading across the room as he relayed Mark's praise from Doll Inc.

Anto swiveled in her chair, facing her colleagues with a vigor that belied the numbers and spreadsheets she was better known for. "Great job, everyone!" she shouted, a rare display of exuberance. "It's a great accomplishment to get feedback from a company like Doll Inc. like this."

Tony leaned back in his chair, accepting the acknowledgment with a nod and a small, knowing smile. "It looks like the framework is working," he said with understated grace.

Tony built on the moment's momentum. "We need to celebrate," he said, his eyes sweeping across the faces before him.

Aldy paused just long enough for curiosity to take root before he continued. "And not just us here in this room—we need to celebrate as a company."

Every pair of eyes widened at the implication of his words, hungry for what was next. Anto furrowed her brow, her business acumen flaring with intrigue. "What do you mean?" she asked.

Without missing a beat, Aldy stood taller and let his vision for their future unfold before them. "We got to scale this; we need to make this our core business model." His hand sliced through the air as if carving out their path forward. "Transform Holt into a solutions company."

The room held its breath.

"Bake this customer-centric culture into Holt's DNA," Aldy finished with conviction.

The energy in the room shifted from celebration to exhilaration as Aldy's words sank in. The framework wasn't just an experiment; it was to become their new reality.

Aldy leaned forward, the glow from his laptop illuminating his determined features. He clicked open a document, and an intricate org chart materialized on the screen for all to see. The bold lines and boxes sketched out a future where roles and responsibilities had shifted and the familiar terrain of their corporate structure had been redrawn to nurture a solutions-oriented culture.

"Before I shoot this over to HR, I need your eyes on it," Aldy said, his voice carrying the weight of imminent change.

Anto shifted in her chair, her gaze lingering on the chart as if searching for cracks in its foundation. "Are you set on pushing this through right away?" she asked, her tone revealing a blend of caution and concern.

Aldy nodded, but Anto wasn't convinced. She remembered past restructuring efforts—the ripples they sent through departments, the morale that took hits, and the productivity that temporarily dipped as employees grappled with new realities.

"The idea has merit," Anto conceded, "but let's not forget how these shake-ups have played out before. We've seen teams buckle under less."

Across the table, Tony's silence was a presence of its own. He sat motionless, his eyes scanning each proposed change like a strategist contemplating a battlefield. He recognized the boldness in Aldy's plan but remained guarded, aware of the unease it could sow among staff already wary of change.

Audrey's analytical gaze moved from box to box, attempting to envision how each shift would play out in reality. The chart before her was more than just a diagram; it was a map leading Holt into uncharted territory. She could sense the potential but also the pitfalls that lay hidden in the transition.

"It makes sense to me," she finally said, her voice betraying a hint of reluctance. She understood the necessity but couldn't shake off the doubt nibbling at her confidence. The sweeping overhaul seemed almost too aggressive for an organization steeped in tradition and predictability.

The room was thick with apprehension; they all grasped the concept intellectually but grappled with it emotionally. Aldy's vision required more than just organizational adjustments—it demanded a leap of faith from every person at Holt.

Despite their reservations, they found themselves nodding along. The allure of progress was undeniable, yet none could entirely dismiss the trepidation that accompanied such sweeping reformations.

Aldy observed their reactions—a mix of support tinged with skepticism—and knew he stood at a crossroads. To hesitate might mean missing their chance to lead rather than follow; to act might stir turmoil within Holt's ranks.

In that moment of shared uncertainty, Aldy made his choice. He would shoulder the risk and shepherd his company through this metamorphosis.

"We're doing this," he declared with resolve that bordered on defiance. "It's time we stop playing it safe."

The team left the conference room carrying a cocktail of excitement and concern—a potent brew that would fuel their journey toward reinvention or lead them into tumultuous waters.

***

The morning sun poured through the vast windows of the Holt headquarters, casting long shadows across the freshly organized conference room. Aldy surveyed his domain, his gaze resting on the new layout of cubicles and offices beyond the glass wall. It was a visual testament to his latest directive—a sweeping reorganization that would dismantle the traditional silos of Holt's past.

He unveiled a bold organizational chart, with each division crafted around clusters of technology and industry-specific solutions. The Software Development and IT Services teams had now morphed into focused groups like 'Retail Innovation' and 'Health-Tech Solutions.' His plan was for these clusters to foster expertise, tailoring their approach to the nuances of each sector. This move demanded an infusion of new talent—solution specialists with experience in both tech and the corresponding industries they now served.

"These specialists," Aldy articulated to his leadership team, "will be our bridge builders. They will stand on the frontier between what we can do technologically and what our clients need for their business."

The air buzzed with muted keystrokes and soft murmurs as teams acclimated to their new roles, their screens awash with the vibrant interfaces of their respective industries.

To cultivate an agile mindset and customer-centric culture, Aldy introduced culture coaches into the mix. These experts dissected Holt's current practices, infusing methodologies from agile frameworks that championed adaptability and rapid response to change. They implemented strategies like sprint planning sessions and daily stand-ups, shrinking the distance between idea conception and execution.

"Culture isn't changed through edict; it evolves through action," one coach would often say as they worked alongside teams, guiding them in real-time through challenges and celebrating small victories that embodied this cultural shift.

Central to this transformation was customer involvement in decision-making. Clients were no longer distant entities at the end of a service or product pipeline; they became active participants in shaping solutions. Holt established advisory boards consisting of customers who would offer feedback at critical junctures, ensuring that every product evolved from real-world insight and need.

The corridors echoed with fresh slogans from internal campaigns aimed at igniting a collective spirit among employees. Posters declaring "Innovate Together" and "Our Clients, Our Co-Creators" adorned walls next to monitors scrolling testimonials from staff about their early successes with client collaborations.

Training sessions were mandatory, but they weren't dry lectures or tedious seminars. Instead, they were interactive workshops where employees role-played scenarios with mock clients or collaborated on rapid prototyping challenges. The importance of these sessions couldn't be overstated—they served as incubators for the behaviors and skills necessary in this new landscape where agility reigned supreme.

Aldy believed knowledge was the cornerstone of change. As such, he invested in extensive training programs covering everything from emerging technologies to empathy in customer service. "We can't just tell our teams to be different; we must equip them with the understanding and tools to live out this change," he often reminded his leaders.

Through these deliberate actions—reorganizing teams around solutions, bringing culture coaches onboard, involving customers in decision-making, launching internal campaigns, and conducting training sessions—Aldy didn't just aim to alter Holt's structure or strategy; he sought to transform its very soul. The metamorphosis was daunting but necessary if Holt was to not only survive but thrive in an industry where stagnation meant obsolescence.

Under the glow of the new dawn, Audrey sat across from Tej in the stark modernity of Holt's conference room. Charts and projections adorned the walls, but their focus was on a singular goal: redefining Holt's image in the marketplace.

"We've got to make it clear—we're not just pushing products; we're curating solutions," Audrey insisted, her hands punctuating each word as if carving them into the very air.

Tej nodded, his eyes scanning the plethora of data points. "We solve problems; that's our narrative now. Every message we craft, every event we sponsor—it all circles back to the customer's needs."

Their campaign unfurled across California, with billboards capturing attention with bold questions about common business headaches and Holt's tailored answers. Radio spots filled the airwaves with testimonials from satisfied clients, while local events turned into stages for Holt's transformation.

A basketball game in Sacramento pulsed with energy, not just from the on-court action but from Holt's presence as well. Their sponsored halftime show—a symphony of drones forming dynamic patterns—mirrored their message: coordinated solutions for complex problems.

Customers took notice. A local retailer struggling with inventory management discovered Holt's branding at a 5K charity run. A booth at the finish line showcased a bespoke retail analytics platform. They later credited this chance encounter for streamlining their operations and boosting profits.

Meanwhile, within Holt's glass walls, Audrey orchestrated a seismic shift in sales culture. She gathered her team, their faces a mix of curiosity and concern as she unveiled Neoteric's framework and the accompanying compensation structure.

"Commissions are no longer tied to sheer volume," she announced. "We reward insight, integration, and impact now."

Murmurs rippled through the room; brows furrowed as calculators clicked—a symphony of unease. Sales executives balked at numbers that didn't promise immediate returns like their old models did.

"But how does this benefit us?" one voice cut through the confusion.

Audrey met the challenge head-on. "Because when our clients thrive, so do we. It's about longevity—repeat business through genuine partnerships."

Training sessions followed, where sales narratives transformed into collaborative discussions about client aspirations and hurdles. Role-plays replaced product pitches with solution conversations.

As weeks turned into months, initial frustration gave way to understanding. Executives began seeing deeper relationships forming with clients—contracts extended and portfolios expanded.

One seasoned sales director shared his epiphany at a quarterly meeting. "I was skeptical; I admit it," he said, his once-resistant tone now brimming with excitement. "But my clients—they're seeing us differently. We're not vendors; we're visionaries to them now."

Incentives started aligning with successful solution implementations rather than up-front sales, and slowly but surely, satisfaction settled among the team like dusk upon the valley—quietly changing the landscape without fanfare but with undeniable presence.

Audrey stood back as her team adapted and overcame initial hurdles—each success reinforcing her belief that Holt was not just changing its branding but was on the cusp of changing an industry mindset—one solution at a time.

Christina surveyed the vast expanse of Holt's engineering department, a sprawling labyrinth of talent and technology waiting to be channeled into something greater. With meticulous care, she began to lay the groundwork for centers of excellence—specialized teams dedicated to mastering specific domains of technology and business solutions.

These centers would become the crucible where expertise was honed, innovation sparked, and new solutions forged.

She started by defining what these centers of excellence were: groups within an organization established to cultivate knowledge, promote best practices, and provide exceptional expertise in a focused area. These teams would serve as repositories of invaluable skills and insights, offering guidance to the rest of the company.

Each center revolved around a dual-axis framework: one axis for technological mastery such as AI, blockchain, or IoT; the other for domain-specific knowledge in sectors like finance, healthcare, or retail. This structure ensured that the solutions developed were not only technologically advanced but also finely tuned to industry-specific challenges.

Christina meticulously selected leads for each center based on a blend of proven expertise and potential for growth. She sought individuals who were not only technically proficient but also visionary in their approach to problem-solving. The chosen leads would be responsible for building their teams, guiding them through new technological landscapes, and aligning their efforts with Holt's overarching strategy.

Training sessions became a staple under Christina's directive. She introduced her engineers to emerging technologies that promised efficiency and cost reduction. For example, she organized workshops on serverless computing, which could speed up deployment times and reduce infrastructure costs. Engineers practiced building microservice architectures that allowed businesses to scale rapidly without hefty upfront investments.

As Christina convened with her engineering team managers, she emphasized the imperative of constructing technology solutions anchored in real-world customer problems.

The initial response was resistance—without explicit requirements from clients, how could they commit resources to learning new technologies or crafting reference architectures?

Christina listened patiently before presenting a compelling report from a leading consulting firm. It outlined imminent trends and breakthrough technologies reshaping the industry landscape—technologies Holt's engineers needed to embrace if they were to become advisors trusted by their clients.

"Look at this," Christina said firmly, tapping on the report's graph depicting rising demand for cloud-native services. "Our customers may not articulate these needs yet, but they will. And we must be ready—not just to respond but to lead."

The managers exchanged skeptical glances until, one by one, realization dawned upon them. They understood that staying ahead meant investing in their team's education and capabilities. Reluctance gave way to resolve as they agreed to spearhead this transformation.

With the larger structure in motion, Christina turned her attention to a more targeted project—the formation of an innovation team tasked with creating internal tools that exemplified Holt's commitment to outcome-based solutions. This elite group embarked on developing a dynamic pricing tool as their maiden venture.

This advanced statistical model tool they were crafting would harness historical data, project complexity metrics, and solution-specific variables to calculate accurate costs dynamically. It would factor in customer use cases and desired outcomes—streamlining quotes and ensuring competitive pricing.

Christina oversaw every aspect with an eagle's eye. She encouraged her team to integrate machine learning algorithms capable of refining cost estimates with each new data point. The tool was designed not just as an internal asset but as a showcase piece—a testament to Holt's ability to innovate from within.

As dusk painted the sky in hues of closure, Christina stood before her teams—architects of tomorrow's solutions—and knew they had set forth on a path not just towards advancement but towards becoming pioneers their customers could rely upon for insights and direction in an ever-evolving tech landscape.

***

Anto leaned back in her leather chair, her gaze sweeping across the array of spreadsheets and charts that wallpapered her monitor. The numbers whispered secrets of cost and revenue, a language she'd mastered over her tenure at Holt. It was time to translate that language into a new dialect, one that spoke of value and outcomes rather than mere transactions.

She summoned a meeting with a select group of financial analysts and strategists, handpicked for their acumen and innovative thinking. In the hushed confines of the conference room, Anto stood at the helm, her presence as commanding as the tailored suit she wore.

"We're shifting gears," Anto announced, tapping the marker on the whiteboard. "Our clients are no longer just buying products; they're investing in outcomes. Our pricing model must reflect that."

The team nodded, understanding the gravity of their task. They poured over Audrey's earlier presentation on "Neoteric," dissecting its phases and how they could be quantified into a customer's success metrics.

One analyst suggested an idea that resonated immediately. "Let's consider a tiered pricing structure," he proposed, drawing circles on the whiteboard that soon turned into a pyramid. "We offer packages – basic to premium – each promising escalating levels of outcome assurance."

Another chimed in, excitement lacing her voice. "And we include performance bonuses tied to key milestones within those outcomes."

Anto's eyes lit up at this proposition. They were crafting an architecture where clients could scale their investment based on their desired level of engagement and anticipated results. This wasn't just selling; it was partnering for success.

As they delved deeper, the team unraveled the complexities of each solution's lifecycle costs. They mapped out customer journeys, pinpointing where Holt's involvement would make tangible impacts on efficiency or growth. Each solution morphed into a menu of possibilities – analytics optimization here, an increase in customer retention there – all measurable, all billable.

They devised an innovative framework to charge customers based on outcomes by establishing clear metrics from the onset. If Holt could reduce a client's operational costs by 15%, for example, part of their fee would hinge on achieving that benchmark.

The analysts devised models that factored in Holt's cost-to-serve alongside projected customer gains. They looked at historical data, market trends, and competitor pricing strategies to calibrate their own. Anto insisted on simulations for various scenarios, ensuring their model could withstand market fluctuations and client variances.

The culmination was an intricate but coherent pricing structure dubbed "ValueScape." It was an adaptive framework with levers and dials fine-tuned to reflect each client engagement's unique value proposition.

In presenting ValueScape to Aldy and the rest of the leadership team, Anto stood confident but clear about the risks and rewards this approach carried.

"This is about alignment," she explained. "Our financial success becomes directly tied to our clients' operational victories."

Audrey nodded from across the table, seeing how this tied back to her own vision for Neoteric. Tony scribbled notes furiously, while Christina considered implications for future tech deployments.

ValueScape wasn't just a pricing model; it was a declaration of Holt's commitment to its clients' successes and its own evolution in a competitive landscape. It was Anto's steadfast resolve carved into Holt's strategy – unyielding yet attuned to change.

***

In the heart of Holt's bustling headquarters, Audrey commandeered the conference room, her eyes reflecting the morning sun's promise as she spread her blueprints across the table. She leaned in, engaging her team with a fervor reserved for visionaries on the verge of change.

"We're at the helm of a sea change here," Audrey began, her voice firm yet inviting. "We've got our sights set on a partner program that'll redefine how we scale and penetrate markets untouched by our hands alone."

She outlined the initiative with meticulous precision. "Our partner program, akin to those of the cloud titans, will be a four-tiered system: Registered, Silver, Gold, and Platinum. It starts with basic benefits for entry-level partners and escalates to exclusive incentives for our top-tier allies."

Tony interjected with a smirk, "And how do you propose we climb this partnership ladder?"

"A combination of sales performance, certifications, and customer success stories," Audrey responded without missing a beat. "Each tier unlocks more resources from us: co-marketing funds, dedicated support, even lead sharing. But they've got to earn it."

"And what about these partners? How do they grow with us?" Tony pressed on.

Audrey gestured toward a graph she'd drawn earlier. "Think of it this way—'A Rising Tide Lifts All Boats.' As Holt innovates and expands, our partners ride the wave with us. They leverage our solutions to grow their own businesses while expanding our reach."

She paused for effect before diving into the funding mechanism—a strategic move designed to cement partnerships. "We're committing significant funds to kick-start their ventures with our solutions. This isn't just seed money; it's an investment in joint success."

Anto raised an eyebrow. "And the criteria for these funds?"

"Tailored to each partnership," Audrey replied confidently. "We evaluate their business model, market strategy, and potential to scale with us. We're not just handing out checks; we're building ecosystems."

Audrey's vision captivated the room as she delved into how technology partners would benefit from bundling their software products with Holt's offerings. "Our solutions become turn-key when combined with theirs—rapid deployment for customers craving efficiency."

"And smaller consulting firms?" Christina asked softly.

Audrey nodded. "They bring niche accelerators we lack—gems that can shine under Holt's brand. Some will go exclusive, becoming ambassadors of our mission."

Tony leaned back in his chair, arms folded across his chest. "This could catapult them into deals they only dreamt of."

"Precisely," Audrey said with a smile.

The conversation shifted to impact—how this strategy didn't just spell growth for Holt but nurtured small businesses into thriving enterprises. They spoke of community impact and brand loyalty.

"As we grow, so does our network—a mosaic of innovation and ambition," Audrey concluded.

Her team exchanged looks of approval and anticipation; they recognized that through this partner program, Holt wasn't merely growing—it was sowing seeds for a forest of opportunity where every sapling had its place in the sun.

In the hush of the morning, before the clamor of the day began, Audrey settled into the conference room with her sales team arrayed around her. Charts and screens lit up the space, a tangible sign of their mission: to carve out Holt's future in the tech solutions market.

Audrey started by laying out their goal. "We're not just selling products; we're selling outcomes. We need to understand our clients' aspirations and align our solutions to help them get there," she explained, tapping a pen against her notepad.

She then turned to the task at hand—building a robust prospect list. "Let's begin with our launch size. We need to map out who's who in this industry and prioritize them based on potential," she instructed.

The team nodded, eyes fixed on their laptops, as they sifted through industry reports and databases. Audrey oversaw the process, ensuring they didn't just chase big names but aligned with companies that shared their vision for innovation.

"Take Luminar Tech," she said, pointing at a mid-sized enterprise on the screen. "They're not Fortune 500, but they're agile and hungry for change—ripe for our solutions."

The room buzzed with activity as they profiled each company, categorizing them into tiers based on Total Addressable Market (TAS). They examined company sizes, market shares, and growth trajectories. The list took shape—a hierarchy of prospects ready for a Holt transformation.

Next, Audrey collaborated with business development to ensure this wasn't a one-off exercise but an ongoing endeavor. She introduced a dynamic system that continually fed new data into their prospect database. The method was efficient—lessons from Doll

Inc.'s implementation guided their strategy, helping them fine-tune their approach with real-world insights.

With the prospect list in place, Audrey turned her attention to revenue goals. She needed a strategy that translated customer aspirations into tangible targets for Holt.

She found Aldy in his office, sunlight framing him as he reviewed reports from recent market analysis. Without hesitation, she presented her question about setting revenue goals.

Aldy looked up, his response swift and clear. "Customer goals become our goals," he stated. "Let's look at each customer and figure out their objectives for the next three years."

He pulled up a whiteboard and began to sketch out his thoughts. "If we're their strategic partner," Aldy continued, "we need to assess what our contribution would be towards achieving those objectives."

Together they brainstormed how this approach could work. They considered a hypothetical client—Innovatech—a company aiming to cut operational costs by 20% over three years through digital transformation.

"If we can provide Innovatech with solutions that contribute directly to their cost-saving goals," Audrey mused aloud, "we can tie our pricing model to those outcomes."

Aldy nodded in agreement. "Exactly," he said. "We'll base our fees on what Innovatech is willing to invest in technology solutions that deliver those savings."

They worked through different scenarios for various clients, outlining how Holt's services could impact each company's ambitions—from increasing market share to enhancing customer experience or reducing time-to-market for new products.

As they mapped out each customer's goals and Holt's role in achieving them, a clear picture emerged: by setting revenue targets grounded in customer success metrics, Holt would transform from vendor to vital ally in their clients' journeys.

This shift would also redefine how Holt measured its own success—not by traditional sales metrics alone but by how effectively they empowered customers to reach new heights.

As they wrapped up their session, Audrey felt energized by the possibilities ahead. With a clear framework to guide them and Aldy's strategic vision lighting the way, Holt was poised not just to meet the future but to shape it alongside their customers.

CHAPTER 9: ALDY'S BIG VISION

REVOLUTIONIZING TOMORROW

The grand hall of Holt's headquarters buzzed with an undercurrent of eager speculation, as employees from various departments converged into a collective huddle. The cavernous space, framed by towering steel columns and expansive panes of glass, thrummed with life as the workforce exchanged speculative whispers and curious glances.

Natural light spilled generously into the room, bathing the assemblage in a warm glow that seemed to pulse with the energy of impending change. The gentle tapping of footsteps on marble echoed through the air, a subtle rhythm underscoring the atmosphere of shared expectancy.

Amid the casual chatter, Aldy made his way to the center of the room, his presence like a magnet pulling their focus. Employees shifted in their seats, craning their necks to catch a glimpse of their CEO, the architect of Holt's impending metamorphosis. The anticipation was palpable, a living thing that filled the room as surely as the air they breathed.

A simplicity marked Aldy's approach—no fanfare or ceremony, just a resolute figure approaching the makeshift stage at the head of the room. A hush fell over the crowd as he ascended the steps, his poised silhouette sharply outlined against the bright backdrop of the morning sun streaming in.

With the staff's attention now undivided, Aldy took his position before the gathered, their collective gaze an unspoken mandate. Behind him was Holt's past—storied and solid—and in front was the untold narrative of its future, about to be unfurled by his guiding hand.

He arrived at the podium and surveyed the sea of faces before him—eager, uncertain, and hopeful. The soft hum of the HVAC system filled brief moments of stillness as he organized his thoughts. He reached for the microphone; its surface was cool and solid beneath his fingertips.

"Good morning," Aldy began, his voice steady and clear. It carried across the room, reverberating off walls lined with achievements past and banners that heralded those yet to come.

Aldy paused, allowing his gaze to meet those of his colleagues—a silent acknowledgment of their shared journey. He sensed their curiosity transforming into focus and their restlessness into readiness.

He clasped his hands in front of him, leaning slightly toward them—a gesture that drew everyone closer. "We stand at a crossroads," he continued, "not just as a company but as architects of our own future."

Aldy's presence filled the room, every word painting a vision more vivid than any corporate directive could capture—a testament to the power that lay not in figures or forecasts but in human potential unleashed.

The crowd leaned in as if drawn by an invisible tide. Aldy stood before them not merely as their CEO but as the embodiment of what they all strived to become—agents of change in an ever-shifting landscape.

And as he prepared to speak again, they waited—poised on the edge of their seats—for what they knew would be not just a speech but a call to action that would resonate through every level of Holt's reimagined identity.

The stage was set under the warm glow of stage lights, casting an aura of expectancy across the room filled with Holt's employees. Aldy stood at the podium, his posture embodying the very confidence and vision he was about to share. He surveyed the crowd, his gaze touching each face as if to beckon them personally into his narrative.

"Ladies and gentlemen of Holt," Aldy began, his voice carrying the unmistakable timbre of purpose, "today I speak not just as your CEO, but as a fellow dreamer who sees a future so bright it outshines the neon buzz of Times Square. I envision a Holt that stands tall and proud—a beacon of innovation and prosperity—not just for the next quarter or the next decade, but beyond a century."

A hush fell over the crowd, and a collective breath held in anticipation.

"Imagine a future where our children, and their children after them, find not just employment but a calling within these walls. Picture a company so integral to our community that it uplifts not only those who wear its badge but also those who merely speak its name."

He paused, letting the imagery settle in their minds.

"This isn't just about business growth; it's about nurturing the very soil we stand on—enriching our local economy, enhancing lifestyles, and fortifying the nation's economic backbone."

Aldy leaned forward slightly, his eyes earnest and intense.

"But how do we get there? It starts with belief. A conviction that runs deep into our culture; a shared vision that ignites passion and drives hard work. It's about doing right by our customers even when no spotlight shines on us—when the only witness is the pride in our craft."

The employees shifted in their seats, his words striking chords within them.

"Each day should begin with this vision—every interaction with customers, every moment we support our colleagues. It's about embracing change, not as an enemy but as an ally. Small shifts in our approach today lay the groundwork for monumental leaps tomorrow."

He raised his hand as if to physically push against resistance.

"Yes, it means having those tough conversations—making decisions that might weigh heavy on our hearts but promise a brighter dawn. And it's about empowerment—igniting that spark within each one of you to reach heights you've never imagined."

The air in the room seemed to be filled with possibility.

"This transformation won't come with a snap of fingers or by flipping a switch. It is a culture—a belief system we'll embed into Holt's very foundation."

Aldy's voice has softened now, inviting intimacy.

"It starts when each one of you believes in your own potential, because when you do, you lift Holt along with you. We are a tapestry woven from individual threads—each one vital to the strength and beauty of what we create together."

He spread his arms wide as if to encompass every soul in attendance.

"I ask for your help on this journey—to 'Believe in YOU.' Let that belief be your guiding star as we sail into uncharted waters toward horizons aglow with promise."

Aldy stepped back from the podium. His closing words hung in the air like a challenge—a call to action echoing through each heart and mind in attendance.

"Together, we can ensure that Holt is not just surviving but thriving beyond 100 years—a legacy etched not in stone but in lives touched and futures forged. Join me; let us build this dream into reality."

As applause thundered through the room, it was clear that Aldy had struck more than just a chord—he had lit a flame within each employee that would grow into an inferno of change and progress for Holt.

Aldy stood before the gathered faces, their attention undivided, their spirits rallying to his call. A hush of anticipation fell over the room as he articulated the path ahead.

"Over the next three years," Aldy began, his voice carrying the gravity of their shared mission, "our objective is to not only elevate Holt but to be the catalyst for transformation for our top ten customers. They are teetering on the brink of obsolescence in this digital era. We have a duty, a responsibility to guide them into a future rich with potential."

He let his gaze wander across the room, making eye contact with each member of his team as if imparting a personal challenge.

"We're setting forth on a bold journey. It demands more than what we've given before—it requires an innovation foundation that is rock solid." Aldy paused, allowing his words to resonate. "This isn't just about business; it's about evolution—yours, mine, ours."

He paced slightly, hands clasped behind his back.

"To achieve this monumental task," he continued, "each of you will work with your managers to craft your own action plan. This isn't merely a corporate roadmap; it's a blueprint for personal and professional growth."

Aldy reached for a glass of water on the podium, taking a sip before placing it back with precision.

"In six months' time," he projected clearly, "I expect to see development in your leadership skills, technical expertise—whatever area you need to master. By twelve months, those skills should be second nature. And in eighteen months, you will be leading others to do the same."

The room remained silent but charged with new energy.

"Remember," Aldy implored, "you can't pour from an empty cup. It's imperative that each of you excel in your area before we can elevate our clients."

He paused for effect before delivering the final piece of his vision.

"As you transform yourselves," he said with unwavering conviction, "you will then work hand in hand with our customers. Show them that change is not only possible but essential. You'll do this with pride and an unshakeable belief in our ability to help them transform."

The team was captivated by Aldy's passion and clarity of purpose.

"We've built Neoteric for this very reason—to structure this transformation journey. The leadership team and I are here to help you adapt it, deliver results beyond what we've imagined."

Aldy's words echoed off the walls as he concluded his address. His vision was clear and bold—a beacon for the path they would carve together.

CHAPTER 10: LUMINARY CODE

BOLD BET PAYS OFF

Sunlight streamed through the expansive windows of Holt's corporate office, bathing the room in a golden glow as Aldy settled into his chair at the head of the conference table. His team—Audrey, Tony, and others—gathered around him, reports in hand, the air thick with anticipation.

Audrey glanced at Aldy, her eyes reflecting the room's optimism. "Do you remember a while back at the same meeting you were worried about Holt?"

Aldy let out a chuckle, his eyes scanning the pages before him. "We have come a long way," he said, the smile lingering on his lips. "It feels like we are in a different company now."

He leaned back, letting the numbers on the report sink in. "Looking at the growth, we have grown 5x in 2 years, and our pipeline shows we will be easily 10x in the next 3 years."

Tony chimed in from across the table, his voice carrying a sense of pride that resonated with everyone present. "More than the revenue growth, look at our people growth. They enjoy working here. They feel proud to be part of this company." He gestured toward a gleaming trophy displayed prominently on a nearby shelf. "We are the most innovative company of the year in Silicon Valley." The award seemed to validate their efforts, a tangible symbol of their transformation.

"Best Talents wants to work here," Tony continued, mirroring Aldy's earlier sentiments. "You were right, Aldy—the company should focus on being a sustainable and growing environment for the people and families who rely on it. Growth and revenue come automatically."

The room filled with nods of agreement; it was clear that each person around that table had witnessed and contributed to Holt's metamorphosis. They had not only kept pace with industry giants but had outstripped them, crafting an empire where innovation was not just encouraged but expected—a place where every employee felt integral to their collective success.

As they prepared for the stakeholder meeting, Aldy's thoughts lingered on how far they had come and how much further they intended to go. The journey ahead was promising and uncharted, but Holt was ready to navigate it with unwavering determination and an innovative spirit that had become their hallmark.

Anto joined the conference room gathering somewhat late, her arrival cutting through the quiet like a knife. Her searching gaze quickly found Aldy standing by the windowsill, immersed in thought. Noticing the envelope he was holding, she casually queried, "What's the story we're telling the board this time?"

"Customer testimonies," Aldy said, his voice tinged with a hint of sarcasm as he turned from the view outside. "Our story is that we took care of the customer, and they are taking care of us. That's it."

"Beautiful," Anto responded, her eyes narrowing slightly as she considered his words. She studied Aldy's expression, noting the furrowed brow and the way his fingers tapped the envelope. Curiosity piqued by his demeanor, she ventured, "Something on your mind?"

Aldy's eyes flickered to the letter on his desk before returning to meet Anto's inquisitive look. "It's an invitation to speak at a conference," he revealed.

Audrey, who had been silently following the exchange, leaned forward. "Where?" she asked.

"The same conference where all this started—Cloudnext," Aldy explained. He let out a breath he didn't realize he'd been holding. "We've been on the partner program with that cloud company and are named as one of the high-growth partners of the year. They want me to speak at their conference and share best practices."

"That's fantastic," Tony chimed in from across the table, his face brightening with enthusiasm.

Aldy offered a modest smile, though it didn't quite reach his eyes. "What are you thinking?" Tony prodded further.

Aldy turned back toward the window, staring into the distance as if seeking answers in the sprawling Silicon Valley below. "Nothing," he finally replied, though they all knew it was far from true. "Just thinking about the message to share with the world about Holt."

Anto nodded slowly, recognizing Aldy's contemplative mood as a sign of deeper gears turning. He was considering not just what to say but how their story would resonate across an industry where Holt had become both a leader and a learner.

The room settled into thoughtful quietness as each pondered their journey—a testament to customer focus and relentless pursuit of innovation that had brought them this far and promised an even more dynamic future.

***

The air in the auditorium crackled with anticipation as the CEO of the cloud company, his voice carrying an undertone of respect, handed the stage over to Aldy. A murmur of curiosity rippled through the thousands gathered; they leaned forward, eager to listen to the leader of a company that was not yet a household name.

Aldy's stride carried an aura of determined calm as he approached the podium. The spotlight found him, a beacon on stage, casting his shadow across the expectant faces. He paused, surveyed the sea of onlookers, and cleared his throat.

"Good morning," Aldy's voice resonated through the room. "I'm Aldy, CEO of Holt. It's an honor to be here today." He nodded in gratitude as a welcoming applause echoed.

With a click, the screen behind him lit up with a bold title:

"The Luminary Code."

Below it are listed ten leadership principles, each a promise and a commitment from Holt.

- **Honesty & Transparency**

Recognizing the need for change even in times of success.

- **Continuous Learning & Development**

Challenging the status quo, pushing boundaries, and discovering new avenues for improvement.

- **Innovation & Collaboration**

Fostering a culture of experimentation, embracing failure, and generating superior results through teamwork.

- **Structure, Prioritization, & Accountability**

Breaking down ideas into manageable components, testing, and creating a structured approach for adaptability. Recognizing the power of organization.

- **Clarity, Vision, & Purpose**

Setting a transformative vision, inspiring belief, and encouraging employees to think big. Clear communication as a catalyst for positive change.

- **Customer Centricity & Partner Friendly**

Prioritizing customers, engaging them in the process, and transforming partners into collaborative team members for accelerated innovation.

- **Inclusion & Relationships**

Ensuring inclusivity, addressing employee concerns, and fostering a culture of mentorship and friendship for sustained growth.

- **Consistency & Results-Driven**

Consistently delivering messages, iterating vision, and embracing a results-oriented mindset for success in the long-term transformation journey.

- **Analytical Rigor & Simplicity**

Measuring everything systematically, empowering every employee with focused dashboards, and investing in automation for simplicity and efficiency.

- **Ethics & Sustainability**

Building a socially conscious and empathic culture, integrating sustainability into goals, and showcasing care for employees, customers, and the world around us.

***

Aldy paced the stage with easy confidence, the bright lights casting his shadow long across the floor. His voice, a blend of resolve and reflection, reached out to the audience. "I'm not going to go over the presentation and explain each of the principles," he began with a smile that hinted at the journey he was about to share.

My journey at Holt began 13 years ago, and for the last six, I've had the honor of leading from the front. Ah, but the last three years, now, have been the most captivating and enlightening of my career.

Pause, Aldy scans the audience with earnest eyes.

I remember sitting where you are now, just three years ago. There I was, part of the crowd, my mind wrestling with unknowns, my heart seeking answers to questions I hadn't yet formed. It was this very conference that marked a defining turn in my professional life and the destiny of our company. It was here that I realized Holt was on the brink of an evolutionary leap—one we didn't know we needed.

Smiling, Aldy paints a picture with his hands.

This conference—oh, it was a wellspring of insights, the kind that signal a need for transformation. You see, we at Holt, like many of you here, had become comfortable. But through a series of revelations, we came to understand that to achieve greatness, we needed to harness that discomfort.

He walks across the stage, his pace reflecting the unfolding story.

Imagine those historical moments when humanity took great leaps forward. Alexander Graham Bell's telephone, Henry Ford's Model T, Thomas Edison's light bulb. These inventions didn't answer public demands; they were the manifestations of astonishing foresight. The visionaries behind these leaps weren't just giving us what we asked for; they were showing us what was possible.

Aldy's eyes drift, as if looking back through history.

This is what we didn't initially realize at Holt. Our transformation didn't stem from a need that was voiced or a box that required ticking. It came from our precursory analysis—our ability to probe and foresee where we had to innovate and grow.

Lowering his voice, Aldy draws the audience closer with his candor.

I learned one of my most significant lessons on leadership: the true power lies in anticipating the need before it becomes evident to the masses, in hearing that subtle cry for advancement. We began to tune in to the whispers of change, the faint signals from our customers that pointed towards a larger shift.

Aldy positions himself at the center, embodying conviction.

"True leadership is not just about navigating the present; it's about anticipating the future and identifying opportunities before they become apparent to others."

This was a pivotal moment, not just for me, but for Holt.

Connecting one last time with the audience.

So, my message to you today is this: listen closely for the whispers of tomorrow, let that subtle unease guide your path, and trust that within it lies the seeds of greatness for your future.

Aldy paused, his gaze sweeping across the sea of eager faces before him. He let the moment hang, charged with anticipation, then continued with renewed vigor.

"When we began to venture beyond our comfort zone, that's when the true magic happened. Our team, accustomed to a certain way of doing things, found themselves in Las Vegas at a tech conference. There, amidst the bright lights and endless chatter of innovation, we stumbled upon the idea that would change everything for Holt."

He gestured emphatically, drawing the audience into his narrative.

"We discovered a new wave of cloud technology. Not just any cloud technology—this was cutting-edge, something that could transform businesses overnight. It was there we realized our potential to not just follow but lead in this industry."

Aldy leaned forward, hands resting on the podium, his voice earnest and compelling.

"We learned that staying static was more dangerous than taking calculated risks. It was an epiphany. Holt couldn't be a mere participant in the tech world; we had to be the maestros."

A murmur of agreement rippled through the crowd.

"From there, we dove headfirst into Generative AI, bespoke software development—areas we'd never touched before. We began integrating predictive analytics and IoT solutions into our offerings. And let me tell you," Aldy's voice rose with excitement, "the journey from being a reliable vendor to a visionary ally for our clients has been nothing short of exhilarating."

The room filled with nods and murmurs of affirmation.

"So here's my new mantra for you all," Aldy proclaimed, a determined spark in his eye. "Seek relentless evolution, for in its pursuit lies the path to our collective triumph."

The crowd erupted into applause as Aldy's words echoed through the auditorium, resonating with an audience hungry for change and ready to take on the world.

Aldy paced the stage, his presence commanding yet accessible, his voice a steady beacon in the auditorium's vast sea of eager listeners. "And you know what I learned? Humility in leadership is not just about accepting your limitations; it's about the eagerness to grow beyond them. I sought wisdom wherever I could find it—big or small, it didn't matter."

He paused, reflecting on a memory that seemed to fuel his passion. "There was this startup, barely a blip on the industry radar—innovative, scrappy, and driven by a clear vision. They weren't just playing the game; they were rewriting the rules."

The audience leaned in, hanging on his every word.

"They had this... this magnetic culture of experimentation. Failure wasn't a setback; it was celebrated as a lesson learned. And that's when it hit me—the foundation of Holt needed to be built on the bedrock of fearless exploration."

A murmur of understanding rippled through the crowd.

"We were too cautious, too wrapped up in our legacy, to dare greatly. But seeing that startup thrive without the fear of failure gave us the courage to reinvent ourselves—to shift from a fortress of old successes to an incubator for groundbreaking ideas."

Aldy's gaze swept over the crowd, connecting with faces alight with inspiration.

"Our journey at Holt transformed when we began to cultivate a growth mindset, one that embraces change as an ally and not an adversary. We learned to listen—to our customers, our employees, even to those outside our industry—and through listening, we discovered endless avenues for innovation."

He paused again, choosing his next words with deliberate care.

"Every voice holds a story; every story hides a lesson. And if you're willing to listen—to truly hear—the symphony of progress will guide your path."

Aldy leaned forward, his voice cutting through the silence that settled over the auditorium after his opening remarks. "When we at Holt had enough evidence to make a change, we didn't hesitate. We began experimenting, diving headfirst into the waters of innovation, learning to swim alongside our customers."

He paced the stage, hands gesturing as if sculpting the air with his conviction. "Innovation isn't a solitary sprint; it's a relay race. It's about taking action, seeking feedback, and refining our approach until the value shines bright for the customer."

Eyes alight with the fire of his own words, he continued, "We learned that innovation is about creating value by not just solving a problem but by making our customers an integral part of the solution. It's about listening to their needs and developing alongside them."

The crowd leaned in, captivated by Aldy's earnestness. "And here's something crucial we discovered: customers love to be involved. When we reach out with genuine empathy and a clear intent to help, they join us in our quest for innovation."

He paused, allowing the truth of his words to resonate. "Never underestimate the power of making your customers part of your journey. Without the collaboration of our most trusted clients, Holt's path to rapid innovation would have been a path untaken."

Aldy's gaze swept across the sea of faces before him as he delivered his closing thought: "Innovation thrives on inclusion, not isolation."

Aldy stood center stage, his voice echoing with conviction. "When we pinpoint those pivotal innovations, those game-changers, it's on us as leaders to craft a vision that's not just seen but felt. Be fearless, be unwavering, and most importantly, be clear on why we're embarking on this transformation."

He paced slowly, his hands gesturing to underscore his points. "Turning the ship around isn't a spectator sport. It's a collective effort, an all-hands-on-deck call to action. You see, our employees aren't just our greatest asset; they're co-navigators in this journey."

The crowd shifted, absorbing the weight of his words. "Real change—it doesn't spark in the boardroom alone. It ignites at every desk, in every conversation. It's our job to map it out for every team member, connecting the vision to their daily grind."

Aldy paused for effect, making eye contact with faces in the audience. "Show them what's at stake for them personally—why they should be the torchbearers of this new era at Holt, not just bystanders."

He leaned forward slightly, a silent hush falling over the room. "When we walk this path together, when we embrace our collective wisdom and experience, any monumental shift becomes more than bearable—it becomes a seamless transition for us and for the clients who count on our unwavering service."

Aldy straightened up, his presence commanding attention. "Remember though—painting that grand vision isn't enough. We've got to lay it out brick by brick. Show them each ripple their actions will create and prep them for the waves to come."

He took a deep breath before delivering the closing thought that would resonate long after his speech ended. "When inclusivity within our ranks is not just an ideal but a practice, every step toward change is a step shared—and every victory, a victory won together."

Aldy's voice resonated across the auditorium, his presence magnifying with each word. "We discovered the transformative power of collaboration when we embraced our partners as extensions of our team. It was nothing short of an epiphany, seeing them elevate us to realms we never fathomed."

He paced slightly, allowing the weight of his words to settle among the audience. "New doors swung open—doors to untapped markets, innovative collaborations, and astonishing growth. This was the bounty we reaped when we nurtured our partnerships with genuine commitment."

He recalled Holt's initial approach to partnerships, a conservative strategy that seemed prudent at the time. "We always valued our partners, but we kept them at arm's length from our customer interactions. It was as if we were guarding a secret that could only be shared under strict terms."

A change in perspective brought a radical shift in their strategy. "But as we ventured into this new direction, it became crystal clear that our success hinged on our partners' involvement and their growth alongside us."

Aldy gestured expansively, encompassing everyone in the room. "We brought them into every dialogue, supported their initiatives, and invested in their development as much as our own. It was no longer about simply doing business together; it was about thriving together."

His gaze swept over the crowd, locking eyes with many who nodded in understanding. "I urge every organization here today to look beyond mere transactions with your partners. Cultivate your ecosystem of alliances, for it is in this rich soil that the seeds of opportunity sprout and flourish."

Pausing for effect, Aldy found the words that encapsulated his message: "Think of your partner network not just as an ecosystem but as a symphony—each element contributing a unique note to a harmonious masterpiece that could never be achieved solo."

Aldy leaned into the microphone, his voice echoing across the auditorium. "Let me tell you about the power of incremental victories," he said, his gaze sweeping over the crowd. "At Holt, we've come to understand that the mightiest of oaks grow from the smallest acorns. Each small win is a building block, a step closer to our grand aspirations."

He paused, allowing the message to sink in. "Consider our 'Neoteric' initiative. We started with simple conversations, understanding our clients' needs at a granular level. Those discussions were our first wins—insights that became the seeds from which 'Neoteric' sprouted."

Aldy gestured emphatically. "And we didn't just keep those wins to ourselves. We celebrated every single one—whether it was positive feedback from a client or a breakthrough in our technology development. Every success was a chance to energize and motivate our team."

The crowd nodded, some jotting down notes, others simply absorbed in his narrative.

"Consistency was key," Aldy continued. "Every day, we strove for progress, no matter how minor it seemed. Those small victories began to snowball, creating momentum that propelled us forward."

He paused again, his expression serious yet filled with pride. "Now, you might walk through Holt's corridors and see a different kind of energy—a kinetic buzz of activity where every team member knows their contribution matters."

Aldy's hands found their way to his hips as he surveyed the audience with a confident stare. "We shifted our decision-making model to one that is utterly results-driven. It doesn't matter if an idea is as brilliant as the stars—if it doesn't yield results or propel us toward our objectives, we let it go."

The room fell silent as Aldy's words lingered in the air.

"We ingrained this mindset into Holt's very DNA," he declared. "Today, ask any of my team what they're working on and they'll show you more than just enthusiasm—they'll show you data, evidence of their trajectory toward well-defined targets."

Aldy straightened his jacket with a quick tug at the lapels. "This simplicity and clarity remove confusion and doubt at every level of our organization. It allows us all—leaders and employees alike—to focus on what truly matters: seizing new opportunities and delivering outcomes with unmatched speed and precision."

He concluded with a nod, acknowledging the audience's attentive gaze. "At Holt, every day is day one—a fresh start where we remain humble but hungry, grounded but always reaching for those stars."

Aldy leaned into the microphone, his gaze sweeping over the sea of attentive faces. "And folks, we didn't stop at innovation and partnerships. We wanted to cultivate an ecosystem where ethics aren't just a policy; they're a practice."

He paused, letting the weight of his words sink in. "At Holt, we strive to grow not just our bottom line, but a positive culture throughout our organization. A culture where trust is the foundation on which every project is built. Where every team member knows they can rely on their colleagues without hesitation."

A murmur of agreement rippled through the crowd as Aldy continued. "It's about more than just teamwork; it's about empathy. Encouraging every person within Holt to step into each other's shoes—whether they're across the hall or across the country."

He recounted an example, his voice brimming with pride. "Take our 'Code for a Cause' initiative—where our developers volunteer their time to create software solutions for non-profits. It started as a small idea from one of our junior devs, and now it's one of our most impactful programs. It's not just about coding; it's about understanding the challenges these organizations face and using our skills to make a real difference."

The audience nodded, visibly moved by the tangible example of empathy in action.

"And this empathy extends to our customers too," Aldy continued. "We don't just sell solutions; we build relationships. We listen, we adapt, and we ensure that what we deliver genuinely meets their needs."

A softness entered his tone as he shared a personal story from within Holt's walls. "Just last month, when Ella from accounting faced a family emergency, her team didn't skip a beat. They reorganized her workload, ensuring she could take the time she needed without worrying about work piling up."

He looked around the room as he concluded, "That's the kind of support that makes employees feel safe, valued...like they're part of something bigger than themselves. It's why many see themselves at Holt for a lifetime."

The auditorium filled with applause—a testament to a leader who not only envisioned change but had also fostered an environment where it thrived in every aspect of company life.

Aldy stepped away from the podium, his chest swelled with pride as the applause echoed through the auditorium. His eyes scanned the crowd, their faces aglow with inspiration. He recognized the light of change in their expressions, the same light that had sparked within Holt during its darkest hours.

"Let me share with you," Aldy continued, his voice carrying over the clapping as he moved through the crowd, "a story from our own backyard at Holt. There was a time when we measured success in quarterly profits and market shares. But that was a shallow victory. The real success came when we dared to measure it by the smiles of our satisfied customers and the passion of our employees."

He paused by a group of young entrepreneurs hanging on his every word. "We introduced 'Tech Tuesdays'—an open house for innovation where any employee could pitch an idea. The result? A junior developer's concept became our leading security software. It wasn't just about revenue; it was about igniting belief in every individual that they could make a difference."

Aldy walked further, his steps confident and measured. "And relationships? We shifted from transactions to partnerships. When one of our oldest clients faced a tough merger, we didn't see it as a contract renegotiation opportunity. Instead, we stood by them, offering solutions to ease their transition. Today, they're not just clients; they're our advocates."

Nearing another group, he noticed heads nodding in agreement. "And community," he said with a smile, "we started 'Holt Helps'—a program where we dedicate time to local causes. Our teams have developed apps for nonprofits at no cost, empowering them to serve more people effectively."

The audience's enthusiasm was palpable now, their applause intermittent with murmurs of approval.

Aldy reached the edge of the stage again and turned back to face them all. "Friends and family," he declared, "at Holt, we've created an environment where work-life balance is not just a policy but a practice. We celebrate birthdays, anniversaries, and personal milestones because we are more than colleagues—we are a family."

The auditorium filled with cheers and some attendees even stood up in ovation.

"And hope for a better future?" Aldy raised his voice slightly to be heard over the growing noise. "We're investing in education programs that open doors for underprivileged youth to enter tech fields—because our future is shaped by those we lift on our way up."

He returned to center stage as the applause reached its peak.

"This 'Luminary Code' isn't just for Holt," Aldy concluded with conviction. "It's for all of us here today and beyond these walls. It's about building something greater than ourselves—something lasting and luminous."

With that final word, he nodded graciously and exited the stage amidst resounding applause—a man who had not only lit the way but had become a beacon for others to follow on their own transformative journeys.

ABOUT THE AUTHOR

Roajer Gilbert is a business solution architect and a strategist who has spent over 20 years leading large business transformations for organizations ranging from high-growth startups to Fortune 500 companies.

Roajer advises leaders on leveraging emerging technologies and evolving business models to stay competitive. He provides advisory and coaching services across IT modernization, digital transformation, customer experience, and product innovation.

In the past, Roajer held senior innovation and strategy roles at leading technology consultancies. He helped reimagine solutions, experiences, and operations for global corporate clients across industries including manufacturing, financial services, healthcare, retail, and more.

Roajer is passionate about helping established companies reignite their innovative spirit. He believes resilience, calculated risk-taking, and a customer-first mindset are key to turning disruption into opportunities for sustainable growth.

The Luminary Code represents the synthesis of Roajer's experiences and observations guiding organizations through major business transformations and technological shifts. He hopes the book provides real-world insights to fellow leaders through storytelling while inspiring them to become the catalysts of change for building stronger companies ready for the future.

He is based in Carmel, Indiana, but works with customers worldwide. When he is not advising clients, Roajer enjoys hiking, working out, and learning new technologies.